THE ART OF PROFIT

Investing with Creative Intelligence

Shah Rukh

CONTENTS

INTRODUCTION

Welcome to "The Art of Profit: Investing with Creative Intelligence," a journey into the captivating world of investment that embraces the principles of creativity, intelligence, and the mastery of financial prosperity. Just as an artist skillfully crafts a masterpiece, investors have the power to shape their financial destinies with precision, foresight, and a touch of creativity.

In this book, we embark on an exploration of investment strategies that go beyond conventional norms, inviting you to unleash the creative investor within. Here, the canvas of financial opportunities awaits, and we will equip you with the brushstrokes of risk and reward, allowing you to create a personalized investment vision that aligns with your dreams and aspirations.

Throughout the chapters, you will discover the palette of diversification, the art of patience, and the significance of understanding the fundamentals. As you navigate the ever-changing market landscape and embrace contrarian thinking, you will find yourself equipped to capture the momentum and make informed investment decisions with the finesse of a seasoned art connoisseur.

Beyond traditional avenues, we will delve into emerging opportunities, sustainable investing, and the intricacies of asset allocation, all while appreciating the wisdom imparted by legendary investors. We will also venture into the world of alternative investment strategies, data analytics, and technical analysis, empowering you with the tools to make well-informed decisions.

In your journey as a creative investor, we will help you build a masterpiece of a diversified portfolio, balancing risks and rewards, and optimizing for long-term success. We will explore the role of behavioral finance, investment psychology, and the emotional palette, acknowledging the influence of our human nature on investment choices.

As your journey continues, you will find yourself sculpting your financial future with an artful touch, embracing opportunities with an entrepreneur's eye, and weaving philanthropy into your investment journey with grace. We will explore global investment vistas, networking as an artful skill, and the importance of legacy planning, ensuring that your wealth gallery stands as a testament to your vision and values.

Throughout "The Art of Profit: Investing with Creative Intelligence," we celebrate the transformative power of collaboration, the significance of ethical investing, and the wisdom of market veterans. We will inspire you to embrace patience and resilience, even during turbulent times, and explore the elegance of portfolio optimization to refine your financial masterpiece continually.

Whether you are a novice investor seeking to lay a strong foundation or a seasoned financial veteran seeking fresh insights, this book offers a comprehensive and intricate gallery of investment strategies and principles. Through each chapter, we invite you to grow, learn, and evolve as a creative investor, painting a financial landscape that truly represents your unique vision of success.

As you immerse yourself in these pages, remember that investing is not just about numbers and graphs; it is an art that requires creative thinking, passion, and the willingness to embrace change. So, let's begin this artistic journey together, where financial mastery becomes a canvas of possibilities, and your investment decisions become brushstrokes of brilliance.

Welcome to "The Art of Profit: Investing with Creative

Intelligence." The canvas awaits your creative touch, and the journey to financial prosperity has just begun.

CHAPTER 1: UNLEASHING THE CREATIVE INVESTOR WITHIN

Introduction:

In the vast landscape of investing, traditional approaches and well-established strategies have long dominated the scene. However, the world of finance is ever-evolving, and as markets become more complex, investors are discovering the need for a new mindset – one that embraces creativity. This chapter delves into the concept of "Unleashing the Creative Investor Within," exploring how harnessing creative intelligence can lead to innovative, effective, and unconventional approaches to investing.

1. The Call for Creative Intelligence in Investing:

Investing is often viewed as a numbers game, driven by rational analysis and logical decision-making. While these elements are undoubtedly crucial, they may not be enough to navigate the intricacies of modern markets. A call for creative intelligence arises from the recognition that traditional models and linear thinking can be limited, and there is a need to explore innovative solutions to achieve better outcomes.

2. Understanding Creative Intelligence:

Creative intelligence is not limited to artistic expression or imaginative pursuits; it encompasses the ability to think critically, solve problems, and generate novel ideas in various contexts. In the realm of investing, creative intelligence involves thinking beyond conventional boundaries, perceiving patterns that others might overlook, and taking calculated risks that lead to exceptional returns.

3. Embracing Risk and Uncertainty:

Unleashing the creative investor within requires embracing risk and uncertainty. Traditional investors often shy away from risks, seeking safe and predictable investments. However, creative investors understand that, in an ever-changing world, calculated risks can lead to extraordinary opportunities. They balance risk with reward potential and develop the courage to step into uncharted territories.

4. Nurturing Curiosity and Continuous Learning:

Curiosity is the fuel for creative intelligence. Creative investors cultivate a curious mindset, continuously seeking new knowledge and staying informed about market trends, emerging technologies, and global events that could impact their investments. They explore diverse industries, read widely, attend conferences, and engage in discussions with experts to expand their intellectual horizons.

5. Encouraging Diverse Perspectives:

The creative investor values diverse perspectives and actively seeks out viewpoints from different backgrounds, industries, and cultures. By integrating a wide range of insights, they gain a more comprehensive understanding of the market landscape, enabling them to identify unique opportunities and anticipate potential challenges.

6. Integrating Art and Science in Investing:

Combining the art and science of investing is at the core of creative intelligence. While financial analysis and data-driven research provide a strong foundation, the creative investor adds an artistic touch by considering qualitative factors, human psychology, and emotional responses that influence market dynamics.

7. The Power of Intuition in Decision-Making:

Intuition, often dismissed in traditional finance, finds its place in the toolkit of the creative investor. With experience and deep knowledge, intuitive decisions can be powerful allies in making swift and accurate choices when data is scarce or ambiguous.

8. Fostering a Growth Mindset:

The creative investor nurtures a growth mindset, viewing failures and setbacks as opportunities for learning and improvement. They understand that success comes with resilience, adaptability, and the willingness to iterate on strategies.

9. Balancing Rationality and Emotional Intelligence:

While rationality is essential in investment decision-making, emotional intelligence plays a vital role in managing emotions during market volatility. The creative investor develops self-awareness and emotional regulation to prevent impulsive decisions and maintain a disciplined approach to investing.

10. Cultivating a Visionary Approach:

Creative investors envision the future, anticipating market trends and technological disruptions. They invest in companies with transformative potential and support innovations that can shape industries for years to come.

Conclusion:

Unleashing the creative investor within involves a transformational journey, embracing new perspectives, and letting go of rigid paradigms. By combining rationality with creativity, embracing uncertainty, and nurturing a growth mindset, the creative investor can unlock untapped potential and discover new avenues for financial success in the dynamic world of investing. Through continuous learning, innovation, and calculated risks, they navigate the complexities of the market, painting a unique path to prosperity.

CHAPTER 2: THE CANVAS OF FINANCIAL OPPORTUNITIES

Introduction:

Imagine the world of finance as a vast canvas, teeming with colors, shapes, and infinite possibilities. In this chapter, "The Canvas of Financial Opportunities," we embark on a journey to explore the multitude of avenues available to investors. Just as artists create masterpieces on a blank canvas, investors have the opportunity to paint their financial futures with a diverse palette of investment options. From traditional stocks and bonds to alternative assets and emerging markets, this chapter unravels the intricacies of financial opportunities and how investors can navigate this expansive canvas to build a robust and diversified portfolio.

1. The Spectrum of Traditional Investments:

At the core of the canvas lie the traditional investments that have long served as cornerstones for portfolios. Stocks and bonds, along with mutual funds and exchange-traded funds (ETFs), offer investors a range of options to participate in the growth of public and private companies and government entities. We delve into the principles of equity and debt investing, understanding risk and return trade-offs, and the significance of asset allocation.

2. The Evolving Landscape of Alternative Investments:

Beyond the traditional, we explore the expanding world of alternative investments. Private equity, venture capital, hedge funds, and real estate present unique opportunities for sophisticated investors to access less liquid and often higher-return asset classes. We examine the strategies, risk factors, and benefits of incorporating alternative investments into a diversified portfolio.

3. Unveiling the Allure of Commodities:

Commodities, such as precious metals, oil, agricultural products, and industrial materials, offer investors exposure to the physical world's economic fundamentals. This section explores the role of commodities in hedging against inflation and diversifying a portfolio, along with the intricacies of commodity futures and options trading.

4. Delving into Derivatives:

Derivatives represent financial contracts whose value derives from underlying assets. We unravel the complexity of options, futures, swaps, and other derivatives, while also highlighting their use in risk management and speculative trading.

5. Exploring the Currency Market:

Currency trading or forex allows investors to speculate on the value of one currency against another. We examine the forces that drive currency fluctuations, the risks associated with forex trading, and its role in global commerce and investment.

6. The Art of Fixed-Income Securities:

Fixed-income securities, including government and corporate bonds, offer investors regular interest payments and a relatively stable income stream. We explore the intricacies of bond investing, yield curves, credit ratings, and the impact of interest rates on fixed-income portfolios.

7. The Colorful World of International Investing:

The canvas of financial opportunities extends globally, presenting investors with a panorama of international markets. We discuss the benefits and challenges of investing in foreign markets, examining strategies to navigate currency risk, geopolitical factors, and regulatory environments.

8. The Emerging Markets Mosaic:

Emerging markets are vibrant and dynamic, offering potential for high growth but also heightened volatility. This section sheds light on the opportunities and risks of investing in emerging economies, with a focus on diversification and long-term growth prospects.

9. The Technological Revolution and Investment:

In the age of technological advancement, we explore the canvas of opportunities presented by the digital realm. Fintech, blockchain, artificial intelligence, and other disruptive technologies are shaping the future of finance, providing new avenues for investment and transformative economic shifts.

10. Impact Investing: Blending Profit with Purpose:

Impact investing represents a powerful intersection of financial goals and positive societal and environmental impact. We examine the rise of socially responsible investing (SRI) and environmental, social, and governance (ESG) criteria, exploring how investors can align their values with their financial pursuits.

11. The Art of Investing in Yourself:

As the ultimate canvas of financial opportunities, investing in oneself holds immeasurable value. We discuss the importance of education, personal development, and enhancing skills to boost earning potential and long-term financial success.

12. Fine-Tuning Your Financial Palette:

As investors paint their financial futures, this section provides practical guidance on building a diversified portfolio that aligns with individual goals, risk tolerance, and time horizon. We explore the role of asset allocation, rebalancing, and periodic reviews in maintaining a well-crafted financial canvas.

Conclusion:

"The Canvas of Financial Opportunities" unveils the richness and diversity of investment options available to investors. Like skilled artists, investors have the power to create masterpieces on this canvas by strategically blending different colors of assets, adjusting brushstrokes of risk, and envisioning their unique financial visions. By understanding the nuances of various investment vehicles and aligning them with personal objectives, investors can paint a picture of financial prosperity, adapt to changing market conditions, and embrace the ever-evolving world of finance with creativity and confidence. Just as every artwork tells a story, every investment strategy reflects an individual's journey towards financial growth and success.

CHAPTER 3: THE BRUSHSTROKES OF RISK AND REWARD

Introduction:

In the world of finance, risk and reward form the foundational brushstrokes that shape every investment decision. Chapter 3, "The Brushstrokes of Risk and Reward," delves deep into these critical elements, exploring their interconnectedness, understanding different types of risk, and the dynamic relationship between risk and potential returns. By mastering these brushstrokes, investors can create a balanced and informed approach to building portfolios that align with their financial goals.

1. The Nature of Risk:

Risk, in the context of investing, refers to the possibility of losing some or all of the invested capital. Understanding the nature of risk is fundamental to making informed decisions. We explore the distinction between systematic and unsystematic risk, along with the role of uncertainty in financial markets.

2. Risk Tolerance and Investor Psychology:

Each investor has a unique risk tolerance, representing their willingness and ability to withstand fluctuations in the value of their investments. We delve into the factors that shape risk tolerance, the impact of emotions on investment decisions, and the significance of aligning risk tolerance with investment strategies.

3. Measuring Risk: Standard Deviation and Beta:

Risk can be quantified and compared using various metrics.

Standard deviation measures the volatility of an investment's returns, while beta gauges its sensitivity to market movements. We discuss how these measures aid investors in assessing the level of risk in their portfolios.

4. The Efficient Frontier and Portfolio Optimization:

The efficient frontier represents the optimal set of portfolios that offer the highest expected returns for a given level of risk. We explore the concept of diversification and how investors can optimize their portfolios to achieve a balance between risk and reward.

5. Unraveling Market Risk: Systematic Risk Factors:

Systematic risk factors, such as interest rate changes, economic conditions, and geopolitical events, influence the entire market. We analyze how these factors impact investment performance and strategies for managing exposure to systematic risk.

6. Navigating Unsystematic Risk:

Unsystematic risk, also known as specific or idiosyncratic risk, is unique to individual assets or industries. We discuss techniques such as diversification and sector rotation to mitigate unsystematic risk and enhance portfolio stability.

7. The Role of Volatility:

Volatility is a measure of the degree of price fluctuations in an investment. We examine how volatility affects investor behavior, trading strategies, and the use of volatility-based products.

8. The Risk-Return Trade-Off:

The risk-return trade-off dictates that higher potential returns are generally associated with higher levels of risk. We explore how investors can identify their risk appetite, set realistic return expectations, and strike a balance that aligns with their financial objectives.

9. Understanding Tail Risk:

Tail risk refers to the possibility of extreme market movements and rare events. We discuss tail risk hedging strategies and how they can protect portfolios during market downturns.

10. Time Horizon and Risk Management:

Investors' time horizon plays a significant role in risk management. We analyze the impact of investment horizon on risk tolerance, asset allocation, and the importance of long-term planning.

11. Behavioral Biases and Risk Perception:

Investor behavior is often influenced by cognitive biases that can lead to irrational decision-making. We explore common biases like loss aversion, herd mentality, and overconfidence, and how they impact risk perception.

12. Risk Management Techniques:

Effective risk management involves employing various techniques, including stop-loss orders, option strategies, and hedging. We explain how these tools can protect investments and limit potential losses.

13. Leveraging Risk in Investment Strategies:

While risk is often perceived as a negative aspect, certain investment strategies embrace risk to generate higher returns. We discuss risk-parity strategies, leverage, and margin trading as methods of using risk to an investor's advantage.

14. The Role of Insurance and Risk Mitigation:

Insurance products can play a vital role in risk mitigation, providing coverage against unforeseen events and reducing financial vulnerabilities. We examine how insurance complements investment strategies and safeguards against specific risks.

15. Evaluating Risk in Different Asset Classes:

Different asset classes carry varying levels of risk. We analyze the risk profiles of stocks, bonds, real estate, commodities, and alternative investments, offering insights into their role in diversified portfolios.

16. Understanding Credit Risk:

Credit risk refers to the potential of a borrower defaulting on debt obligations. We explore how credit risk assessment is crucial for fixed-income investors and the impact of credit ratings on bond investments.

17. Market Timing and Risk:

Timing the market is a challenging endeavor, and attempting to predict short-term price movements can introduce additional risk. We discuss the pros and cons of market timing and the importance of a long-term perspective.

18. Stress Testing and Scenario Analysis:

Stress testing and scenario analysis are risk management tools that assess the resilience of a portfolio under adverse conditions. We illustrate how these tools help investors prepare for potential worst-case scenarios.

19. Risk-Adjusted Performance Metrics:

Traditional performance metrics may not capture the true risk-adjusted returns of an investment. We explore metrics like Sharpe ratio, Sortino ratio, and Treynor ratio, which evaluate performance relative to risk taken.

20. The Evolution of Risk Management:

As financial markets evolve, risk management techniques evolve too. We examine the history of risk management and how lessons from past crises have influenced modern risk management practices.

Conclusion:

"The Brushstrokes of Risk and Reward" paints a comprehensive picture of the critical role risk plays in the world of investing. Investors can no longer overlook or fear risk but must instead embrace it as an integral part of the canvas that shapes their financial journey. By understanding different types of risk, employing risk management strategies, and aligning risk tolerance with investment goals, investors can achieve a harmonious balance between risk and potential reward. Just as a skilled artist uses precise brushstrokes to create a masterpiece, the art of investing lies in skillfully navigating the canvas of risk and reward to build a robust and successful investment portfolio.

CHAPTER 4: CRAFTING YOUR INVESTMENT VISION

Introduction:

The journey of successful investing begins with a clear and compelling vision. In Chapter 4, "Crafting Your Investment Vision," we explore the process of creating a well-defined roadmap that aligns with an investor's unique goals, aspirations, and values. Just as an artist envisions their masterpiece before putting brush to canvas, an investor must define their financial objectives and outline the steps to achieve them. This chapter delves deep into the art of crafting an investment vision, emphasizing the importance of clarity, purpose, and adaptability in building a robust and fulfilling investment strategy.

1. Understanding the Power of Vision:

A vision serves as the guiding light for every investor. It provides direction, motivation, and a sense of purpose. We discuss the significance of setting a long-term vision that transcends short-term market fluctuations and acts as a foundation for informed decision-making.

2. Identifying Financial Goals:

Crafting an investment vision begins with identifying specific and achievable financial goals. Whether it's retirement planning, purchasing a home, funding education, or leaving a legacy, we explore the process of setting SMART (Specific, Measurable, Achievable, Relevant, and Time-bound) goals that drive investment strategies.

3. Defining Risk Tolerance:

An investment vision is deeply linked to an individual's risk tolerance. We revisit the importance of understanding and aligning risk tolerance with financial goals to create a well-balanced and sustainable investment approach.

4. Assessing Time Horizon:

Time horizon plays a critical role in investment decision-making. We discuss the impact of time horizon on asset allocation, risk management, and the need to adapt strategies based on evolving circumstances.

5. Aligning with Personal Values:

Beyond financial goals, an investment vision incorporates an individual's personal values and ethical considerations. We explore the concept of socially responsible investing (SRI) and how investors can align their investment decisions with their moral compass.

6. Defining the Investment Philosophy:

Every investor has a unique approach to investing, often guided by an investment philosophy. We discuss various philosophies, such as value investing, growth investing, and dividend investing, and how they shape portfolio construction.

7. Embracing Flexibility and Adaptability:

While a vision provides a roadmap, flexibility is essential in the ever-changing landscape of finance. We explore the significance of adaptability in responding to market dynamics, economic shifts, and personal life changes.

8. The Role of Financial Advisors:

Financial advisors play a crucial role in helping investors craft their vision. We discuss the benefits of seeking professional advice, finding the right advisor, and establishing a collaborative relationship.

9. Building an Investment Policy Statement (IPS):

An Investment Policy Statement (IPS) serves as a formal document that outlines an investor's objectives, risk tolerance, asset allocation, and guidelines for portfolio management. We provide a step-by-step guide to creating a comprehensive IPS.

10. Asset Allocation Strategies:

Asset allocation is a key component of crafting an investment vision. We examine various allocation strategies, including strategic, tactical, and dynamic allocation, and how they adapt to different market conditions.

11. The Role of Asset Classes in the Investment Vision:

Understanding the characteristics and risk-return profiles of various asset classes is crucial in crafting an investment vision. We explore the role of stocks, bonds, cash, real estate, and alternative assets in diversified portfolios.

12. Evaluating Investment Vehicles:

Investors have a wide array of investment vehicles at their disposal. We discuss the features and considerations of mutual funds, ETFs, index funds, individual securities, and other investment options.

13. Tax Considerations and the Investment Vision:

Tax efficiency is a significant aspect of an investment vision. We explore tax implications in portfolio construction, tax-efficient investing strategies, and the impact of different account types (e.g., taxable, tax-deferred, tax-free).

14. Rebalancing and Monitoring Progress:

As the investment landscape evolves, rebalancing is crucial in maintaining the alignment with the investment vision. We examine the significance of periodic reviews, portfolio adjustments, and tracking progress toward financial goals.

15. The Psychological Aspect of Investing:

Crafting an investment vision involves managing emotions and avoiding behavioral biases that can lead to impulsive decisions. We explore the psychological challenges of investing and techniques to maintain discipline.

16. The Role of Philanthropy in the Investment Vision:

Investors with a philanthropic mindset may incorporate charitable giving into their investment vision. We discuss donor-advised funds, impact investing, and the fulfillment of creating positive change through investments.

17. Family Legacy and Multi-Generational Planning:

For some investors, the vision extends beyond their own lifetime. We explore the importance of multi-generational planning, preserving family wealth, and passing on values to future generations.

18. The Evolution of the Investment Vision:

An investment vision is not static; it evolves with changing circumstances and life stages. We discuss the process of revisiting and refining the investment vision to adapt to new goals and market conditions.

19. Risk Management in the Investment Vision:

Risk management is an integral part of any investment vision. We examine techniques for hedging risk, using insurance products, and employing prudent risk management strategies.

20. The Impact of External Factors on the Investment Vision:

The investment vision may be influenced by external factors, such as economic trends, geopolitical events, and regulatory changes. We discuss how to stay informed and adjust the vision accordingly.

Conclusion:

Crafting an investment vision is an art that demands introspection, self-awareness, and informed decision-making. By defining clear financial goals, understanding risk tolerance, aligning with personal values, and embracing flexibility, investors can paint a masterpiece of financial success. The investment vision becomes the anchor that guides them through market volatility, economic uncertainties, and life's twists and turns. With a well-crafted investment vision, investors can confidently pursue their dreams and aspirations, secure in the knowledge that their financial decisions are grounded in purpose and guided by a thoughtful and comprehensive strategy. As the canvas of investments unfolds, the investment vision becomes the brushstroke that paints a portrait of a prosperous and fulfilling financial future.

CHAPTER 5: THE PALETTE OF DIVERSIFICATION

Introduction:

In the world of investing, diversification is akin to a versatile artist's palette, offering a broad array of colors to paint a robust and resilient portfolio. Chapter 5, "The Palette of Diversification," delves into the art and science of diversifying investments to reduce risk and enhance potential returns. Just as artists blend different hues to create a captivating masterpiece, investors mix various asset classes, industries, and geographic regions to build a well-balanced and stable portfolio. This chapter explores the principles of diversification, its benefits, and practical strategies for implementing it effectively.

1. Understanding Diversification:

Diversification is the practice of spreading investments across a range of assets to minimize the impact of individual asset performance on the overall portfolio. We discuss the rationale behind diversification, its historical significance, and how it became a cornerstone of modern portfolio management.

2. The Risk-Return Trade-Off and Diversification:

Diversification is directly linked to the risk-return trade-off. We explore how combining assets with different risk profiles enables investors to optimize returns while managing risk more effectively.

3. The Power of Correlation:

Correlation measures the degree to which two or more assets move in relation to each other. We delve into positive and negative correlations and explain how low or negative correlations between assets contribute to effective diversification.

4. Asset Allocation: Building the Foundation:

Asset allocation is the allocation of investments among different asset classes, such as stocks, bonds, cash, and alternative assets. We discuss the significance of asset allocation as the foundation of a diversified portfolio.

5. Equities: The Core of Diversification:

Equities, or stocks, play a significant role in a diversified portfolio. We explore the importance of considering different equity categories, such as large-cap, small-cap, and international stocks, to achieve comprehensive diversification.

6. The Role of Bonds in Diversification:

Bonds are essential components of a diversified portfolio, providing stability and income. We discuss the various types of bonds, including government, corporate, and municipal bonds, and their role in mitigating risk.

7. Cash and Cash Equivalents:

Cash and cash equivalents add liquidity to a portfolio and act as a buffer against market volatility. We examine the role of cash, money market funds, and short-term securities in diversification.

8. The Versatility of Alternative Assets:

Alternative assets, such as real estate, commodities, private equity, and hedge funds, offer unique diversification benefits. We explore their characteristics and considerations for including them in a diversified portfolio.

9. Geographic Diversification:

Investors can diversify across geographic regions to reduce country-specific risks. We discuss the benefits and challenges of international diversification, including exposure to emerging and developed markets.

10. Sector Diversification:

Sector diversification involves investing in various industries to avoid concentration risk. We analyze sector rotation strategies and the impact of economic cycles on sector performance.

11. The Role of Exchange-Traded Funds (ETFs):

ETFs have revolutionized diversification, offering investors access to a wide range of asset classes and sectors. We examine the benefits of using ETFs in portfolio construction.

12. Mutual Funds in Diversification:

Mutual funds pool money from multiple investors to invest in a diversified portfolio. We explore the types of mutual funds and their role in diversification.

13. Diversification and Market Timing:

Diversification is closely linked to market timing. We discuss how attempting to time the market can hinder the effectiveness of diversification and the importance of a disciplined, long-term approach.

14. Rebalancing: Maintaining Diversification:

Over time, the asset allocation of a portfolio may drift from its intended diversification targets. We discuss the significance of regular rebalancing to maintain the desired risk profile.

15. The Impact of Fees on Diversification:

Investment fees can erode portfolio returns, especially in actively managed funds. We explore cost-effective strategies for achieving diversification and the role of low-cost index funds.

16. Achieving Diversification in Taxable and Tax-Advantaged Accounts:

Diversification should be considered across taxable and tax-advantaged accounts. We discuss tax-efficient investment strategies and the role of asset location in portfolio management.

17. Diversification in Retirement Accounts:

Retirement accounts, such as 401(k)s and IRAs, offer unique opportunities for diversification. We explore the selection of investment options and the benefits of tax-deferred growth.

18. Diversification Across Investment Styles:

Different investment styles, such as growth, value, and blend, can enhance diversification. We analyze the characteristics of each style and their contribution to portfolio diversification.

19. Dynamic Diversification in Changing Markets:

Diversification should adapt to evolving market conditions. We discuss dynamic diversification strategies that respond to economic shifts and emerging trends.

20. The Future of Diversification:

As financial markets evolve, the concept of diversification may expand. We speculate on the future of diversification, including the role of artificial intelligence and data analytics in portfolio construction.

Conclusion:

"The Palette of Diversification" presents a vivid canvas of investment possibilities that can lead to a harmonious and resilient portfolio. Diversification, like a skilled artist's palette, empowers investors to blend various asset classes, geographic regions, and investment vehicles to create a well-balanced masterpiece. By understanding the principles of diversification, leveraging correlation, and regularly rebalancing, investors can navigate market fluctuations with confidence. As the investment landscape evolves, diversification remains a timeless and indispensable technique, offering the potential for superior risk-adjusted returns and a colorful investment journey. Through strategic diversification, investors can paint a financial future that weathers the storms of uncertainty and stands as a testament to the art and science of successful investing.

CHAPTER 6: EMBRACING THE ART OF PATIENCE

Introduction:

In the fast-paced world of investing, patience is often an undervalued virtue. Chapter 6, "Embracing the Art of Patience," delves into the profound impact of patience on investment success. Like a skilled artist taking time to craft a masterpiece, patient investors understand that enduring results require a long-term perspective and steadfast resolve. This chapter explores the art of cultivating patience in the face of market volatility, resisting impulsive decisions, and staying committed to a disciplined investment approach.

1. The Essence of Patience in Investing:

Patience is the ability to remain calm and composed while waiting for investment theses to unfold. We discuss the significance of patience as a counterbalance to market turbulence and the role of delayed gratification in achieving financial goals.

2. The Impact of Emotional Discipline:

Patience and emotional discipline go hand in hand. We explore the psychological challenges of investing, the dangers of emotional decision-making, and techniques for maintaining composure during market fluctuations.

3. Understanding the Long-Term Horizon:

Investing with patience requires embracing a long-term horizon. We discuss the benefits of long-term investing, including compounding returns and the advantages of riding out market cycles.

4. The Power of Compound Interest:

Compound interest is a magical force that rewards patient investors. We illustrate the compounding effect and its exponential growth over time.

5. The Art of Contrarian Thinking:

Patience often involves contrarian thinking, going against the crowd when market sentiment is high or low. We discuss the art of being a contrarian investor, with a focus on the importance of independent analysis and avoiding herd mentality.

6. Time in the Market vs. Timing the Market:

The adage "time in the market beats timing the market" underscores the value of patience. We explore the challenges of market timing and the advantages of staying invested over the long haul.

7. Resisting the Fear of Missing Out (FOMO):

FOMO can lead investors to make impulsive decisions, chasing after hot trends. We discuss how patience helps combat FOMO and the benefits of staying disciplined in investment choices.

8. The Patience to Weather Market Volatility:

Markets are inherently volatile, and patience is vital during turbulent times. We discuss strategies for coping with market volatility and how staying patient can lead to favorable outcomes.

9. Embracing the Power of Inaction:

Sometimes, the best action is no action at all. We explore the art of waiting for the right opportunities, resisting unnecessary trading, and avoiding overactivity in a portfolio.

10. Patience in Value Investing:

Value investing, a strategy made famous by Warren Buffett, epitomizes the art of patience. We discuss the principles of value investing, including buying undervalued assets and holding for the long term.

11. The Virtue of Holding onto Quality Investments:

Patience involves holding onto quality investments despite short-term fluctuations. We examine the benefits of staying committed to high-quality assets and businesses.

12. Navigating Through Economic Cycles:

Economic cycles can test an investor's patience. We discuss the art of understanding economic cycles, adjusting investment strategies accordingly, and maintaining a long-term view.

13. The Impact of Patience on Risk Management:

Patience plays a crucial role in risk management. We explore how it helps investors ride out downturns, avoid panic-selling, and remain focused on long-term objectives.

14. The Art of Learning from Mistakes:

Patient investors view mistakes as learning opportunities. We discuss the importance of a growth mindset, embracing failures, and using setbacks as stepping stones to success.

15. Developing a Patient Investment Plan:

Crafting a patient investment plan involves aligning financial goals with the appropriate time horizon. We explore how to tailor a plan to individual needs, risk tolerance, and investment objectives.

16. The Role of Diversification in Patience:

Diversification complements patience in portfolio management. We discuss how diversified portfolios help reduce risk and provide stability during market downturns.

17. Patience and Research in Investing:

Patience is an essential aspect of investment research. We discuss the art of conducting thorough due diligence, seeking quality information, and avoiding rushed decisions.

18. The Role of Financial Education:

Financial education fosters patience by providing a deeper

understanding of investment principles. We explore the benefits of continuous learning and the role of education in shaping patient investors.

19. The Art of Staying Committed:

Patience requires staying committed to a well-crafted investment plan, even during challenging times. We discuss strategies for reinforcing commitment and resisting the temptation to abandon a long-term strategy.

20. The Evolution of Patience in Investing:

As investing evolves, the art of patience may adapt to new challenges. We speculate on the future of patient investing, incorporating technological advancements and shifting market dynamics.

Conclusion:

"Embracing the Art of Patience" portrays patience as the brushstroke that adds depth and endurance to an investor's journey. Patient investors understand that success is not an overnight endeavor, but a masterpiece crafted through thoughtful planning, discipline, and a long-term view. By resisting emotional impulses, staying committed to well-defined goals, and embracing the power of compounding, patient investors can navigate the volatile waters of finance with confidence. The art of patience is a timeless and invaluable asset, a guiding light that helps investors create enduring wealth and achieve their financial aspirations. As the canvas of financial markets unfolds, the art of patience colors the investment landscape, revealing a path to prosperity painted with the strokes of wisdom and resilience.

CHAPTER 7: PAINTING A SOLID FOUNDATION: UNDERSTANDING FUNDAMENTALS

Introduction:

Just as a skilled artist begins a masterpiece with a solid foundation, successful investing relies on a deep understanding of fundamentals. In Chapter 7, "Painting a Solid Foundation: Understanding Fundamentals," we delve into the bedrock of investment analysis, exploring the key principles that underpin sound decision-making. Just as an artist study the elements of form, color, and composition, investors must comprehend the fundamentals of companies, industries, economies, and financial markets. This chapter explores the art of fundamental analysis, emphasizing its role in identifying value, assessing risk, and building a strong investment foundation.

1. The Essence of Fundamental Analysis:

Fundamental analysis is the art of evaluating the intrinsic value of an investment asset. We discuss its significance in understanding the underlying factors that influence asset prices.

2. The Fundamentals of Company Analysis:

Understanding the fundamentals of individual companies is essential for stock investors. We explore financial statements, ratios, and qualitative factors that aid in assessing a company's health and potential for growth.

3. Digging into Earnings and Revenue:

Earnings and revenue are crucial aspects of company

fundamentals. We examine earnings per share (EPS), revenue growth, and their impact on stock valuations.

4. The Art of Valuation: Price-to-Earnings (P/E) Ratio:

The P/E ratio is a fundamental valuation metric. We discuss how it helps investors gauge a company's relative value and assess potential investment opportunities.

5. The Importance of Balance Sheets:

A company's balance sheet reveals its financial health and solvency. We explore the art of analyzing balance sheets to understand a company's assets, liabilities, and equity.

6. Cash Flow Analysis:

Cash flow analysis is a critical element of fundamental research. We discuss cash flow statements and their significance in assessing a company's ability to generate cash.

7. Unraveling Income Statements:

Income statements provide insights into a company's profitability. We explore revenue, expenses, and earnings components, illuminating how they impact investment decisions.

8. Understanding Industry Fundamentals:

Industry analysis complements company analysis. We discuss the importance of studying industry trends, competition, and growth potential.

9. Macroeconomic Fundamentals:

Macro fundamentals encompass broader economic factors that impact financial markets. We explore indicators such as GDP, inflation, and employment, and their relevance to investors.

10. The Role of Interest Rates:

Interest rates are fundamental to economic cycles and financial markets. We examine their influence on asset prices and investment strategies.

11. The Art of Analyzing Economic Indicators:

Economic indicators offer valuable insights into market trends. We discuss leading, lagging, and coincident indicators and their significance in predicting economic conditions.

12. Monetary Policy and Central Banks:

Central banks play a pivotal role in shaping monetary policy. We explore how interest rate decisions and quantitative easing impact financial markets.

13. The Impact of Fiscal Policy:

Fiscal policy, including government spending and taxation, affects economic growth and investment dynamics. We discuss how fiscal measures influence investor sentiment.

14. Global Fundamentals: Understanding Geopolitical Risks:

Global fundamentals encompass geopolitical risks and international events. We analyze their impact on global markets and investors' decision-making.

15. Currency Fundamentals:

Currency analysis is vital for investors with exposure to foreign markets. We discuss factors influencing exchange rates and their effects on international investments.

16. Commodity Fundamentals:

Commodity markets are influenced by supply, demand, and geopolitical factors. We explore the fundamentals of commodities and their role in investment strategies.

17. The Art of Market Sentiment:

Market sentiment is a crucial aspect of fundamental analysis. We discuss how emotions and crowd psychology influence asset prices.

18. The Influence of Analyst Recommendations:

Analyst recommendations can sway investor sentiment. We

examine the art of interpreting analyst reports and the limitations of following consensus.

19. The Importance of Corporate Governance:

Corporate governance is a fundamental consideration for investors. We explore the significance of management quality and ethical practices.

20. The Evolution of Fundamental Analysis:

As financial markets evolve, fundamental analysis adapts to new challenges. We speculate on the future of fundamental analysis, incorporating technology and data analytics.

Conclusion:

"Painting a Solid Foundation: Understanding Fundamentals" portrays fundamental analysis as the bedrock of successful investing. Just as an artist study the elements of their craft, investors must master the art of evaluating company performance, industry trends, and economic indicators. By grasping the fundamentals, investors can make informed decisions, identify opportunities, and navigate market uncertainties with confidence. The solid foundation of fundamental analysis empowers investors to paint a canvas of successful investment portfolios, built on a deep understanding of value, risk, and potential returns. As the investment landscape unfolds, the art of fundamental analysis remains a timeless and indispensable tool, illuminating the path to financial prosperity with knowledge and insight. Through diligent study and meticulous research, investors can create masterpieces of financial success, secured by a strong and informed investment foundation.

CHAPTER 8: NAVIGATING THE MARKET'S EVER-CHANGING LANDSCAPE

Introduction:

Investing in financial markets is akin to traversing an ever-changing landscape. In Chapter 8, "Navigating the Market's Ever-Changing Landscape," we explore the dynamic nature of financial markets, characterized by volatility, technological advancements, regulatory changes, and evolving investor sentiments. Just as an experienced traveler adapts to shifting terrains and weather conditions, successful investors must embrace flexibility, resilience, and continuous learning to navigate the complexities of the market. This chapter delves into the art of anticipating and adapting to market changes, seizing opportunities, and managing risks in an ever-evolving investment environment.

1. The Unpredictable Nature of Financial Markets:

Financial markets are inherently unpredictable. We discuss the impact of market sentiment, news events, and macroeconomic factors on market volatility.

2. Embracing Change as an Investor:

Change is a constant in the market landscape. We explore the art of embracing change, staying adaptable, and recognizing that opportunities often arise amidst uncertainty.

3. The Influence of Technological Advancements:

Technological innovations are reshaping financial markets. We examine the impact of artificial intelligence, big data, and algorithmic trading on market dynamics.

4. Navigating the Rise of Fintech:

Fintech is disrupting traditional financial services. We discuss the emergence of online platforms, robo-advisors, and blockchain technology, and their implications for investors.

5. Regulatory Changes and Investor Impact:

Regulatory shifts can significantly influence market behavior. We explore the art of monitoring regulatory developments and understanding their impact on investments.

6. Globalization and Interconnected Markets:

Financial markets are interconnected globally. We discuss the implications of international trade, capital flows, and geopolitical events on investment strategies.

7. Adapting to Economic Cycles:

Economic cycles impact market performance. We explore the art of adapting investment strategies to thrive in various economic environments.

8. The Art of Anticipating Market Trends:

Anticipating market trends requires analysis and research. We discuss technical analysis, chart patterns, and fundamental indicators that aid in identifying potential market movements.

9. Behavioral Finance and Investor Decision-Making:

Behavioral finance explores how human biases influence investment decisions. We examine the art of recognizing and mitigating cognitive biases to make informed choices.

10. The Role of Market Sentiment:

Market sentiment can sway asset prices. We discuss how investor emotions, sentiment indicators, and crowd behavior impact market movements.

11. Mastering Contrarian Investing:

Contrarian investing involves going against prevailing market sentiment. We explore the art of contrarian thinking and the benefits of identifying opportunities when others fear or flee.

12. The Impact of News and Media on Markets:

News and media shape investor perceptions. We discuss the art of discerning credible information, avoiding hype, and making rational decisions amidst media noise.

13. Understanding Market Bubbles and Crashes:

Bubbles and crashes are recurring phenomena in financial markets. We examine the art of recognizing bubble-like conditions and protecting investments during market downturns.

14. Identifying Emerging Market Trends:

Emerging market trends offer opportunities for growth. We discuss the art of identifying emerging industries, technologies, and global economic shifts.

15. Staying Ahead with Research and Analysis:

Continuous research is essential for investors. We explore the art of conducting due diligence, analyzing financial statements, and monitoring industry trends.

16. The Role of Market Experts and Gurus:

Market experts and gurus influence investor sentiment. We discuss the art of seeking diverse perspectives while avoiding blind reliance on external opinions.

17. The Art of Long-Term Thinking:

Navigating the market's landscape demands a long-term perspective. We explore the benefits of patient investing and resisting short-term distractions.

18. Diversification as a Risk Management Tool:

Diversification helps manage risks in an ever-changing market. We discuss the art of building diversified portfolios that adapt to market conditions.

19. Crisis Management and Market Resilience:

Crises are inevitable in financial markets. We explore the art of crisis management, risk mitigation, and seizing opportunities during downturns.

20. The Future of Market Navigation:

As financial markets evolve, the art of navigation will continue to evolve. We speculate on the future of investing, incorporating emerging technologies, sustainable investing, and global shifts.

Conclusion:

"Navigating the Market's Ever-Changing Landscape" portrays investing as a dynamic journey through ever-changing terrains. Successful investors must embrace adaptability, resilience, and continuous learning to navigate the complexities of the market. By recognizing the unpredictable nature of financial markets, staying informed, and anticipating market trends, investors can seize opportunities and manage risks effectively. The art of navigation empowers investors to adjust their strategies, make informed decisions, and thrive in an ever-evolving investment environment. As the investment landscape continues to transform, the art of navigation remains a timeless and indispensable skill, guiding investors toward their financial goals with wisdom and foresight. Through strategic navigation, investors can paint a canvas of success and create a masterpiece of financial prosperity that endures the test of time.

CHAPTER 9: THE ART OF CONTRARIAN THINKING

Introduction:

In the world of investing, the majority often follows prevailing trends and consensus opinions. However, Chapter 9, "The Art of Contrarian Thinking," explores the power of going against the crowd and adopting a contrarian approach. Just as a skilled artist challenges conventional norms to create unique and thought-provoking art, contrarian investors question popular beliefs to uncover undervalued opportunities and avoid market pitfalls. This chapter delves into the art and psychology of contrarian thinking, emphasizing its role in generating long-term investment success and maintaining independence in decision-making.

1. Understanding Contrarian Investing:

Contrarian investing is the art of challenging conventional wisdom and taking positions contrary to prevailing market sentiment. We discuss the philosophy of contrarianism and its principles in the context of financial markets.

2. The Psychology of Contrarian Thinking:

Contrarian thinking requires understanding behavioral biases that influence investor decisions. We explore the psychological factors that lead to herd mentality and the art of overcoming them.

3. Going Against the Herd:

Contrarians dare to go against the crowd. We examine the art of embracing independent thinking and resisting the fear of missing out (FOMO) in a fast-paced market environment.

4. The Art of Value Investing:

Value investing epitomizes contrarian thinking. We discuss the principles of value investing, including seeking undervalued assets and investing with a margin of safety.

5. Contrarian Perspectives on Market Bubbles:

Contrarians challenge the exuberance of market bubbles. We explore the art of recognizing and avoiding speculative bubbles that can lead to severe market downturns.

6. Identifying Oversold and Overbought Conditions:

Contrarian investors seek opportunities in oversold and overbought market conditions. We discuss the art of identifying when market sentiment has reached extremes.

7. The Role of Sentiment Indicators:

Contrarian thinking leverages sentiment indicators. We explore the art of using indicators like the Fear and Greed Index to gauge investor sentiment and market extremes.

8. Contrarianism and Market Timing:

Contrarian thinking intersects with market timing. We discuss the art of using contrarian signals to identify potential market turning points.

9. The Art of Selective Disagreement:

Contrarians may selectively disagree with consensus opinions. We explore the art of conducting independent research and forming well-informed opinions.

10. Contrarian Perspectives on Media Influence:

Media plays a significant role in shaping investor sentiment. We discuss the art of critically evaluating media reports and avoiding emotional reactions to news.

11. The Challenge of Being a Lone Wolf:

Contrarian investors often stand alone. We explore the art of maintaining conviction in contrarian positions despite opposition.

12. The Art of Patience in Contrarian Investing:

Contrarian thinking demands patience. We discuss the art of waiting for the market to recognize the value of contrarian positions.

13. Contrarian Strategies in Different Market Conditions:

Contrarians adapt to various market conditions. We explore the art of applying contrarian strategies in bull markets, bear markets, and volatile environments.

14. Navigating Contrarian Strategies in Political Events:

Contrarian investors navigate political events with prudence. We discuss the art of assessing the impact of political changes on investments.

15. Contrarianism in Behavioral Finance:

Behavioral finance explains the rationale behind contrarian thinking. We explore the art of recognizing cognitive biases and using them to advantage.

16. Contrarian Perspectives on Momentum Investing:

Contrarian thinking challenges momentum investing. We discuss the art of avoiding herd behavior in momentum-driven markets.

17. Seeking Opportunities in Unpopular Industries:

Contrarians seek value in unpopular industries. We explore the art of identifying undervalued sectors and overlooked companies.

18. The Art of Differentiating between Noise and Signals:

Contrarian investors distinguish between market noise and significant signals. We discuss the art of focusing on relevant information to make informed decisions.

19. Contrarian Perspectives on Market Analysts:

Contrarians question market analysts' consensus. We explore the art of formulating independent assessments and understanding potential biases.

20. The Evolution of Contrarian Thinking:

Contrarian thinking continues to evolve with changing market dynamics. We speculate on the future of contrarian investing, incorporating technology and new investment vehicles.

Conclusion:

"The Art of Contrarian Thinking" celebrates the spirit of independence and critical thinking in investing. Just as a visionary artist challenges norms to create groundbreaking works, contrarian investors defy herd mentality to identify unique opportunities. By understanding the psychology of market sentiment, leveraging value investing principles, and staying patient, contrarian investors can paint a canvas of success that endures market fluctuations. The art of contrarian thinking empowers investors to make rational, independent decisions, uncover hidden gems, and avoid speculative traps. As the investment landscape evolves, contrarian thinking remains a timeless and indispensable skill, fostering resilience, discipline, and long-term success. Through contrarianism, investors can create masterpieces of financial prosperity, guided by a thoughtful and unique perspective that stands out amidst the noise of consensus. Contrarian investing becomes the brushstroke that adds depth and originality to an investor's journey, painting a portrait of wisdom, courage, and success in the ever-changing landscape of financial markets.

CHAPTER 10: INVESTING IN TECHNICOLOR: EXPLORING TECHNOLOGY OPPORTUNITIES

Introduction:

The world of technology has revolutionized virtually every aspect of our lives, and the investment landscape is no exception. In Chapter 10, "Investing in Technicolor: Exploring Technology Opportunities," we embark on a journey through the vibrant and dynamic world of technology investing. Just as a painter uses a wide array of colors to create a masterpiece, investors can explore the diverse spectrum of technology opportunities to build a forward-looking and diversified portfolio. This chapter delves into the art of identifying innovative technologies, understanding disruptive trends, and seizing opportunities in the rapidly evolving tech sector.

1. The Technology Revolution:

The technology revolution has transformed industries, economies, and societies. We discuss the impact of technological advancements on investment opportunities.

2. Exploring Technology Sectors:

The technology sector encompasses a diverse range of industries. We explore sectors such as information technology, artificial intelligence, biotechnology, clean energy, and more.

3. The Art of Identifying Disruptive Technologies:

Investing in technology involves identifying disruptive innovations that can reshape markets. We discuss the art of recognizing transformative technologies early on.

4. The Role of Research in Technology Investing:

Research is crucial in understanding complex technology opportunities. We explore the art of conducting thorough due diligence and analyzing emerging trends.

5. Understanding Technology Cycles:

Technology cycles can be swift and transformative. We discuss the art of navigating technology booms and busts while maintaining a long-term perspective.

6. The Impact of Regulation on Technology:

Regulation plays a role in shaping technology markets. We explore the art of assessing the impact of regulatory changes on technology investments.

7. The Art of Investing in Startups and Venture Capital:

Investing in startups and venture capital involves risk and potential reward. We discuss the art of assessing early-stage opportunities and diversifying risk in this space.

8. Exploring Artificial Intelligence and Machine Learning:

Artificial intelligence (AI) and machine learning are driving innovation. We explore the potential of AI in various industries and its impact on investment opportunities.

9. Embracing the Internet of Things (IoT):

The IoT connects devices and unlocks new possibilities. We discuss the art of identifying investment opportunities in the rapidly expanding IoT landscape.

10. The Potential of Cloud Computing:

Cloud computing has revolutionized data storage and processing. We explore the art of investing in cloud-based technologies and the companies leading this space.

11. The Role of E-commerce and Digital Payments:

E-commerce and digital payments have transformed retail. We

discuss the art of investing in this evolving space, including payment processors, fintech companies, and online retailers.

12. The Rise of Clean Energy and Sustainability:

Clean energy and sustainability are gaining prominence in the investment landscape. We explore the art of investing in renewable energy, electric vehicles, and green technologies.

13. The Potential of Biotechnology and Healthcare Innovation:

Biotechnology is driving breakthroughs in healthcare. We discuss the art of investing in biotech companies and the potential of healthcare innovation.

14. The Influence of 5G and Connectivity:

5G technology is set to transform connectivity. We explore the art of investing in 5G infrastructure and related technologies.

15. The Art of Investing in Cybersecurity:

Cybersecurity is a critical aspect of the technology landscape. We discuss the art of investing in companies addressing the growing need for digital security.

16. The Potential of Augmented and Virtual Reality:

Augmented and virtual reality are expanding beyond entertainment. We explore the art of investing in this immersive technology.

17. The Impact of Quantum Computing:

Quantum computing holds promise for revolutionary advancements. We discuss the art of investing in companies at the forefront of quantum computing.

18. The Role of Big Data and Data Analytics:

Big data and data analytics drive informed decision-making. We explore the art of investing in companies leveraging data-driven insights.

19. The Art of Investing in Technology ETFs:

Technology ETFs offer diversified exposure to the tech sector. We discuss the art of selecting technology-focused ETFs for investment portfolios.

20. The Future of Technology Investing:

The technology landscape will continue to evolve. We speculate on the future of technology investing, including emerging trends and disruptive innovations.

Conclusion:

"Investing in Technicolor: Exploring Technology Opportunities" celebrates the boundless potential of technology in investment portfolios. Just as a painter creates vibrant and multifaceted artworks, investors can explore the rich spectrum of technology opportunities to create diverse and forward-looking portfolios. By identifying disruptive technologies, conducting thorough research, and understanding market cycles, investors can seize opportunities in the dynamic world of technology. The art of technology investing empowers investors to be part of transformative innovations and capitalize on the growth potential of cutting-edge industries. As the technology landscape continues to expand and reshape the world, investing in technicolor becomes a timeless and indispensable strategy for long-term investment success. Through strategic technology investments, investors can paint a canvas of financial prosperity, colored by the vibrancy and innovation of the ever-evolving tech sector. Investing in technicolor becomes the brushstroke that adds depth, excitement, and growth to an investment journey, creating a masterpiece of technological prowess and financial resilience.

CHAPTER 11: THE ELEGANCE OF SUSTAINABLE INVESTING

Introduction:

Sustainable investing, also known as socially responsible investing (SRI) or environmental, social, and governance (ESG) investing, represents a transformative shift in the world of finance. In Chapter 11, "The Elegance of Sustainable Investing," we embark on a journey through the world of sustainable investing, exploring how investors can align their financial goals with social and environmental values. Just as a skilled artist crafts an elegant masterpiece, sustainable investing seeks to create a more sustainable and equitable world while generating long-term financial returns. This chapter delves into the art of incorporating environmental, social, and governance factors into investment decisions, promoting responsible corporate practices, and contributing to a brighter and more sustainable future.

1. Understanding Sustainable Investing:

Sustainable investing encompasses a range of investment approaches that integrate environmental, social, and governance factors into decision-making. We discuss the essence of sustainable investing and its rise in popularity.

2. The Foundations of ESG: Environmental, Social, and Governance Criteria:

ESG criteria are the building blocks of sustainable investing. We explore the environmental factors, social considerations, and corporate governance principles that guide sustainable investment choices.

3. The Art of Values-Based Investing:

Values-based investing allows investors to align their portfolios with their personal values and beliefs. We discuss the art of incorporating ethical considerations into investment decisions.

4. The Role of Impact Investing:

Impact investing seeks to generate positive social and environmental outcomes alongside financial returns. We explore the art of measuring and assessing the impact of investments.

5. Sustainable Development Goals (SDGs) and Responsible Investing:

The United Nations' SDGs offer a framework for sustainable development. We discuss the art of incorporating SDGs into investment strategies.

6. The Elegance of ESG Integration:

ESG integration involves incorporating ESG factors into traditional investment analysis. We explore the art of integrating ESG considerations without sacrificing financial performance.

7. Sustainable Investing Strategies:

Sustainable investing offers various strategies, including exclusionary screening, positive screening, thematic investing, and engagement. We discuss the art of selecting the most suitable strategies.

8. The Financial Materiality of ESG Factors:

ESG factors can impact financial performance. We explore the art of identifying financially material ESG considerations that influence investment outcomes.

9. The Art of Corporate Engagement:

Engagement involves actively communicating with companies to promote sustainable practices. We discuss the art of engaging with corporate management and driving positive change.

10. The Influence of Shareholder Activism:

Shareholder activism empowers investors to influence corporate policies. We explore the art of using shareholder rights to advocate for sustainability and responsible governance.

11. ESG Ratings and Data Analytics:

ESG ratings provide insights into company performance. We discuss the art of interpreting ESG data and its role in investment decision-making.

12. The Integration of Climate Change Considerations:

Climate change is a significant driver of sustainable investing. We explore the art of incorporating climate change considerations into investment strategies.

13. The Impact of Sustainable Investing on Risk Management:

Sustainable investing can enhance risk management. We discuss the art of mitigating ESG-related risks and building resilient portfolios.

14. Sustainable Investing and Long-Term Value Creation:

Sustainable investing emphasizes long-term value creation. We explore the art of fostering sustainability-driven growth and profitability.

15. The Art of Constructing ESG-Focused Portfolios:

ESG-focused portfolios require thoughtful construction. We discuss the art of building diversified and impact-oriented investment portfolios.

16. Sustainable Investing and Financial Performance:

Studies show that sustainable investing can lead to competitive financial performance. We explore the art of balancing financial objectives with sustainable goals.

17. The Rise of Green Bonds and Sustainable Debt

Instruments:

Green bonds and sustainable debt instruments fund environmentally friendly projects. We discuss the art of investing in these instruments.

18. The Role of Corporate Reporting and Transparency:

Transparency is critical for sustainable investing. We explore the art of evaluating corporate reporting and ensuring accountability.

19. The Art of Investing in Socially Responsible Mutual Funds and ETFs:

Socially responsible mutual funds and ETFs provide accessible sustainable investment options. We discuss the art of selecting and evaluating these funds.

20. The Future of Sustainable Investing:

Sustainable investing continues to evolve. We speculate on the future of sustainable finance, including emerging trends and evolving practices.

Conclusion:

"The Elegance of Sustainable Investing" celebrates the beauty of integrating social and environmental values with financial objectives. Just as an elegant piece of art conveys meaningful messages, sustainable investing seeks to create positive change while achieving financial prosperity. By incorporating ESG criteria, promoting responsible corporate practices, and engaging with companies, investors can contribute to a more sustainable and equitable world. The art of sustainable investing empowers investors to shape a better future, aligning their portfolios with their values and supporting the advancement of sustainable development goals. As the world embraces the elegance of sustainable investing, the impact of responsible finance will continue to reverberate across industries and societies. Sustainable investing becomes the brushstroke that adds depth, purpose, and elegance to an investment journey, creating a masterpiece that not only stands the test of time but also leaves a lasting legacy of positive impact for generations to come.

CHAPTER 12: BALANCING ACT: MASTERING ASSET ALLOCATION

Introduction:

Asset allocation is the cornerstone of successful investing, much like the careful balance of colors in an artist's palette. In Chapter 12, "Balancing Act: Mastering Asset Allocation," we explore the art and science of allocating investments across different asset classes to achieve optimal risk-adjusted returns. Just as a skilled artist chooses the right blend of colors to create a harmonious painting, investors must carefully select a mix of assets to construct portfolios that align with their financial goals, risk tolerance, and time horizon. This chapter delves into the art of asset allocation, considering factors such as diversification, risk management, market cycles, and investor objectives.

1. Understanding Asset Allocation:

Asset allocation refers to the distribution of investments among different asset classes, such as stocks, bonds, cash, real estate, and alternative investments. We discuss the significance of asset allocation in achieving portfolio objectives.

2. The Role of Risk and Return:

Asset allocation is influenced by the trade-off between risk and return. We explore the art of balancing risk and reward to meet investment objectives.

3. The Art of Diversification:

Diversification is a fundamental principle of asset allocation. We discuss the art of spreading investments across various assets to reduce risk and enhance returns.

4. Strategic vs. Tactical Asset Allocation:

Strategic asset allocation involves setting long-term target allocations, while tactical asset allocation involves adjusting positions based on market conditions. We explore the art of combining these approaches.

5. The Impact of Investment Time Horizon:

Investment time horizon influences asset allocation decisions. We discuss the art of tailoring portfolios to short-term, medium-term, and long-term financial goals.

6. Considering Risk Tolerance:

Investors have different risk tolerances. We explore the art of aligning asset allocation with individual risk profiles.

7. The Role of Modern Portfolio Theory (MPT):

Modern Portfolio Theory guides asset allocation by emphasizing the importance of diversification and the efficient frontier. We discuss the art of applying MPT principles to portfolio construction.

8. The Influence of Market Cycles:

Market cycles impact asset performance. We explore the art of adapting asset allocation to prevailing market conditions.

9. The Art of Asset Allocation in Retirement Planning:

Asset allocation is critical for retirement planning. We discuss the art of constructing portfolios that balance growth and income during retirement.

10. The Impact of Economic Indicators:

Economic indicators influence asset allocation decisions. We explore the art of incorporating macroeconomic factors into investment strategies.

11. Asset Allocation Strategies for Tax Efficiency:

Tax efficiency is crucial in asset allocation. We discuss the art of minimizing tax implications through strategic asset placement.

12. The Art of Rebalancing:

Rebalancing involves adjusting portfolio allocations to maintain desired asset weights. We explore the art of disciplined and systematic portfolio rebalancing.

13. Asset Allocation in Different Market Environments:

Asset allocation strategies vary in different market environments. We discuss the art of adapting allocations in bull markets, bear markets, and periods of uncertainty.

14. The Role of Asset Class Correlations:

Asset class correlations impact portfolio risk. We explore the art of selecting assets with low correlations to achieve diversification benefits.

15. Asset Allocation in Global Markets:

Global markets offer diverse investment opportunities. We discuss the art of asset allocation in international and emerging markets.

16. The Art of Combining Active and Passive Strategies:

Active and passive investment strategies can complement each other. We explore the art of blending active and passive investments in asset allocation.

17. Evaluating Asset Classes and Investment Vehicles:

Investors have numerous asset classes and investment vehicles to choose from. We discuss the art of evaluating and selecting suitable assets.

18. The Art of Dynamic Asset Allocation:

Dynamic asset allocation involves adjusting portfolios based on changing market conditions. We explore the art of tactical allocation in response to market trends.

19. The Influence of Behavioral Finance on Asset Allocation:

Behavioral biases impact asset allocation decisions. We discuss the art of overcoming cognitive biases in portfolio construction.

20. The Future of Asset Allocation:

Asset allocation techniques will continue to evolve. We speculate on the future of asset allocation, incorporating new investment opportunities and technological advancements.

Conclusion:

"Balancing Act: Mastering Asset Allocation" celebrates the art of constructing well-balanced and diversified investment portfolios. Just as a skilled artist achieves harmony and cohesion in their work, investors can attain financial harmony through effective asset allocation. By considering factors such as risk, return, time horizon, and individual preferences, investors can create portfolios that align with their unique financial goals. The art of asset allocation empowers investors to navigate market uncertainties, seize opportunities, and achieve long-term financial success. As the investment landscape evolves, mastering asset allocation remains a timeless and indispensable skill, guiding investors to create portfolios that reflect their vision and aspirations. Through thoughtful asset allocation, investors can paint a canvas of financial prosperity, blending colors of growth, stability, and resilience, to create a masterpiece of investment success that endures the test of time.

CHAPTER 13: THE ARTISTRY OF VALUE INVESTING

Introduction:

Value investing is a timeless and revered approach to investing, akin to the artistry of a master painter. In Chapter 13, "The Artistry of Value Investing," we embark on a journey through the principles and philosophy of value investing. Just as an artist carefully examines the nuances of light and shadow to create depth in their work, value investors analyze financial markets to identify undervalued assets and opportunities. This chapter delves into the art of value investing, exploring the wisdom of legendary investors, fundamental analysis, and the quest for intrinsic value.

1. Understanding Value Investing:

Value investing is a strategy that seeks to identify undervalued assets trading below their intrinsic worth. We discuss the essence of value investing and its appeal to patient and contrarian investors.

2. The Philosophy of Benjamin Graham:

Benjamin Graham, the father of value investing, laid the groundwork for the artistry of value investing. We explore Graham's principles, including the margin of safety and the concept of Mr. Market.

3. The Influence of Warren Buffett:

Warren Buffett, a disciple of Graham, exemplifies the art of value investing. We discuss Buffett's approach to value investing, his focus on quality companies, and his emphasis on a long-term perspective.

4. The Art of Fundamental Analysis:

Fundamental analysis is at the core of value investing. We explore the art of analyzing financial statements, assessing a company's intrinsic value, and identifying potential investment opportunities.

5. The Role of Price-to-Earnings (P/E) Ratio:

The P/E ratio is a fundamental valuation metric in value investing. We discuss the art of using P/E ratios to gauge a company's relative value and potential for growth.

6. The Art of Contrarian Thinking:

Value investors often take contrarian positions. We explore the art of going against prevailing market sentiment to uncover undervalued assets.

7. The Quest for Intrinsic Value:

Value investing seeks to determine a company's intrinsic value. We discuss the art of estimating intrinsic value based on cash flow, earnings, and asset valuation.

8. The Margin of Safety Principle:

The margin of safety is a cornerstone of value investing. We explore the art of investing with a margin of safety to protect against downside risk.

9. The Art of Evaluating Management Quality:

Value investors assess management quality. We discuss the art of analyzing leadership, corporate governance, and ethical practices.

10. The Influence of Dividend Investing:

Dividend investing aligns with the principles of value investing. We explore the art of selecting dividend-paying companies for long-term investment.

11. The Art of Identifying Undervalued Stocks:

Value investors seek undervalued stocks with growth potential. We discuss the art of screening for value opportunities using quantitative and qualitative factors.

12. Value Investing in Different Market Environments:

Value investing strategies adapt to market conditions. We explore the art of applying value investing principles in bull markets, bear markets, and periods of uncertainty.

13. The Impact of Behavioral Finance on Value Investing:

Behavioral biases influence investor decisions. We discuss the art of overcoming cognitive biases in value investing.

14. Value Investing and Market Timing:

Value investors do not attempt market timing. We explore the art of staying patient and focusing on long-term value.

15. The Art of Value Investing in Bonds:

Value investing extends to the bond market. We discuss the art of seeking undervalued bonds with attractive yields.

16. Value Investing in Real Estate:

Value investing principles apply to real estate investments. We explore the art of identifying undervalued properties and income-generating opportunities.

17. The Role of Economic Moats:

Value investors look for companies with sustainable competitive advantages. We discuss the art of identifying economic moats that protect a company's profitability.

18. The Influence of Price-to-Book (P/B) Ratio:

The P/B ratio is another key valuation metric in value investing. We explore the art of using P/B ratios to assess a company's book value relative to its market price.

19. The Art of Portfolio Construction:

Value investors build diversified portfolios. We discuss the art of constructing balanced portfolios with a mix of undervalued assets.

20. The Future of Value Investing:

Value investing continues to evolve. We speculate on the future of value investing, incorporating technology, ESG considerations, and emerging investment opportunities.

Conclusion:

"The Artistry of Value Investing" celebrates the timeless principles and wisdom of value investing. Just as a master painter creates depth and richness in their art, value investors analyze financial markets to uncover hidden gems and undervalued opportunities. The art of value investing empowers investors to make well-informed decisions, guided by fundamental analysis and a focus on long-term value. As the investment landscape evolves, the artistry of value investing remains a steadfast and indispensable approach, instilling discipline, patience, and a commitment to intrinsic worth. Through value investing, investors can paint a canvas of financial prosperity, enriched by the wisdom of legendary investors, the rigor of fundamental analysis, and the resilience of a patient and contrarian mindset. Value investing becomes the brushstroke that adds depth, resilience, and wealth to an investment journey, creating a masterpiece of enduring financial success and lasting wealth for generations to come.

CHAPTER 14: CAPTURING MOMENTUM: RIDING MARKET TRENDS

Introduction:

Capturing momentum in the financial markets is akin to riding a powerful wave as it surges forward. In Chapter 14, "Capturing Momentum: Riding Market Trends," we embark on a thrilling journey through the world of momentum investing, where investors seek to profit from the persistence of price trends and market sentiment. Just as a skilled surfer anticipates and rides the crest of a wave, momentum investors identify and capitalize on assets experiencing significant price movements. This chapter delves into the art of momentum investing, exploring momentum indicators, technical analysis, and the behavioral factors driving market trends.

1. Understanding Momentum Investing:

Momentum investing is a strategy that capitalizes on the momentum of asset prices. We discuss the essence of momentum investing and its appeal to short-term traders and trend-followers.

2. The Power of Market Trends:

Market trends can be potent and enduring. We explore the art of identifying and riding trends to maximize investment returns.

3. The Role of Momentum Indicators:

Momentum indicators track the strength and direction of price movements. We discuss the art of using indicators like Moving Average Convergence Divergence (MACD), Relative Strength Index (RSI), and Stochastic Oscillator to assess momentum.

4. The Art of Technical Analysis:

Technical analysis is foundational to momentum investing. We explore the art of analyzing price charts, patterns, and trends to inform investment decisions.

5. The Momentum Factor in Factor Investing:

Momentum is a key factor in factor investing models. We discuss the art of integrating momentum into factor-based portfolios.

6. The Influence of Behavioral Finance on Momentum:

Behavioral biases impact momentum investing. We explore the art of recognizing cognitive biases in market participants and their influence on trends.

7. Riding Market Trends in Different Asset Classes:

Momentum investing applies to various asset classes, including stocks, bonds, commodities, and currencies. We discuss the art of capturing momentum across diverse markets.

8. The Art of Trend-Following Strategies:

Trend-following strategies underpin momentum investing. We explore the art of adhering to price trends and setting clear entry and exit points.

9. The Impact of Market Sentiment:

Market sentiment drives momentum. We discuss the art of gauging investor sentiment through sentiment analysis and market sentiment indicators.

10. The Art of Scaling-In and Scaling-Out:

Momentum investors practice scaling-in and scaling-out of positions. We explore the art of gradually building and reducing exposure to manage risk and optimize returns.

11. The Role of Price Action Trading:

Price action trading complements momentum investing. We discuss the art of using price patterns and candlestick charts to inform trading decisions.

12. The Impact of News and Events on Momentum:

News and events can trigger momentum shifts. We explore the art of assessing news-driven momentum and its implications for investment strategies.

13. The Art of Risk Management in Momentum Investing:

Risk management is crucial in momentum investing. We discuss the art of setting stop-loss orders and managing position sizes to control risk.

14. The Influence of Algorithmic Trading:

Algorithmic trading impacts momentum in financial markets. We explore the art of navigating momentum-driven algorithms.

15. Capturing Momentum in Short-Term vs. Long-Term Investments:

Momentum investing spans short-term and long-term horizons. We discuss the art of applying momentum strategies to various investment timeframes.

16. The Art of Combining Momentum with Other Investment Approaches:

Momentum can be combined with other investment styles. We explore the art of blending momentum with value investing, growth investing, and other strategies.

17. Capturing Momentum in Bull and Bear Markets:

Momentum strategies adapt to different market conditions. We discuss the art of capturing momentum in both bullish and bearish market environments.

18. The Role of Exchange-Traded Funds (ETFs) in Momentum Investing:

Momentum-focused ETFs offer accessible exposure to momentum strategies. We explore the art of selecting and evaluating momentum ETFs.

19. The Art of Behavioral Momentum Investing:

Behavioral momentum investing seeks to exploit behavioral biases in market participants. We discuss the art of identifying and capitalizing on momentum-driven behavioral patterns.

20. The Future of Momentum Investing:

Momentum investing continues to evolve. We speculate on the future of momentum strategies, incorporating technological advancements and emerging market trends.

Conclusion:

"Capturing Momentum: Riding Market Trends" celebrates the art of recognizing and riding the powerful currents of market trends. Just as a skilled surfer harnesses the energy of the waves, momentum investors identify and capitalize on the momentum of asset prices. The art of momentum investing empowers traders and investors to embrace trends, make timely decisions, and optimize returns in dynamic market environments. As the investment landscape evolves, capturing momentum remains a timeless and adaptable strategy, guided by technical analysis, momentum indicators, and behavioral insights. Through momentum investing, traders and investors can paint a canvas of financial success, capturing the energy and direction of market trends to create a masterpiece of trading prowess and profitable investment decisions. Capturing momentum becomes the brushstroke that adds excitement, agility, and profitability to an investment journey, creating a mosaic of strategic agility and financial gains that endures the test of time.

CHAPTER 15: THE FINE ART OF BEHAVIORAL FINANCE

Introduction:

Behavioral finance is a fascinating and intricate field that delves into the human psychology and emotions that influence financial decision-making. In Chapter 15, "The Fine Art of Behavioral Finance," we embark on an enlightening journey through the realm of behavioral finance, exploring the cognitive biases, heuristics, and emotional factors that shape investor behavior. Just as an artist pays attention to the finest details in their work, understanding the intricacies of behavioral finance allows investors to navigate the complexities of the financial markets with greater awareness and insight. This chapter delves into the art of behavioral finance, unraveling the mysteries of investor behavior and the implications for investment strategies.

1. Understanding Behavioral Finance:

Behavioral finance examines the psychological and emotional factors that influence financial decisions. We discuss the essence of behavioral finance and its contribution to understanding market anomalies.

2. The Role of Behavioral Biases:

Behavioral biases are the cognitive shortcuts that impact decision-making. We explore the art of recognizing common biases such as overconfidence, loss aversion, and confirmation bias.

3. The Influence of Prospect Theory:

Prospect theory explains how individuals assess risk and make choices. We discuss the art of understanding prospect theory and its impact on investment decisions.

4. The Art of Emotional Intelligence in Finance:

Emotional intelligence plays a role in financial decision-making. We explore the art of managing emotions, avoiding impulsive behavior, and maintaining discipline in investing.

5. The Impact of Herd Mentality:

Herd mentality drives market movements. We discuss the art of recognizing and avoiding the influence of the herd in investment decisions.

6. The Art of Mental Accounting:

Mental accounting affects how individuals categorize and treat money. We explore the art of overcoming mental accounting biases to make rational financial choices.

7. The Influence of Anchoring and Adjustment:

Anchoring biases involve reliance on initial information. We discuss the art of avoiding the anchoring effect in investment analysis.

8. The Role of Availability Heuristic:

Availability heuristic leads to decision-making based on readily available information. We explore the art of seeking diverse information to avoid availability bias.

9. The Art of Contrarian Thinking in Behavioral Finance:

Contrarian thinking challenges behavioral biases. We discuss the art of using contrarian approaches to navigate market sentiment.

10. The Influence of Regret Aversion:

Regret aversion impacts decision-making. We explore the art of managing regret and avoiding reactive investment choices.

11. The Art of Framing Effects:

Framing effects influence how information is presented and

perceived. We discuss the art of recognizing framing biases in financial contexts.

12. The Impact of Overtrading and Undertrading:

Overtrading and undertrading are behavioral pitfalls. We explore the art of achieving a balanced and disciplined trading approach.

13. The Art of Investor Education and Empowerment:

Investor education is essential in overcoming biases. We discuss the art of promoting financial literacy and empowering investors to make informed choices.

14. The Influence of Social Proof:

Social proof drives investment decisions. We explore the art of making independent judgments despite social influence.

15. The Art of Goal-Directed Investing:

Goal-directed investing aligns with behavioral finance principles. We discuss the art of setting clear financial goals and designing investment strategies accordingly.

16. The Role of Feedback Loops:

Feedback loops impact investor behavior. We explore the art of learning from past decisions and adjusting strategies accordingly.

17. The Art of Understanding Prospectuses and Disclosures:

Disclosure documents contain vital information. We discuss the art of reading prospectuses and understanding potential biases.

18. The Impact of Excessive Optimism and Pessimism:

Excessive optimism and pessimism affect market sentiment. We explore the art of maintaining a balanced perspective in dynamic market conditions.

19. The Art of Behavioral Finance in Trading Strategies:

Behavioral finance informs trading strategies. We discuss the art of incorporating behavioral insights into trading approaches.

20. The Future of Behavioral Finance:

Behavioral finance will continue to evolve. We speculate on the future of behavioral finance, incorporating advancements in neuroscience and technology.

Conclusion:

"The Fine Art of Behavioral Finance" celebrates the intricate interplay between human psychology and financial decision-making. Just as an artist masterfully weaves emotions and perception into their work, understanding behavioral finance empowers investors to navigate the financial markets with greater self-awareness and resilience. The art of behavioral finance allows investors to recognize cognitive biases, manage emotions, and make rational choices in a world of irrationality. As the investment landscape evolves, behavioral finance remains a timeless and indispensable tool for understanding investor behavior and market anomalies. Through the lens of behavioral finance, investors can paint a canvas of financial success, blending the rationality of analysis with the richness of human emotions and perceptions to create a masterpiece of profitable investment strategies and wise financial choices. The fine art of behavioral finance becomes the brushstroke that adds depth, insight, and self-awareness to an investment journey, creating a mosaic of prudent decision-making and enduring financial prosperity for generations to come.

CHAPTER 16: SCULPTING YOUR INVESTMENT PORTFOLIO

Introduction:

Creating an investment portfolio is akin to sculpting a work of art, where each asset is carefully chosen and positioned to form a cohesive and balanced whole. In Chapter 16, "Sculpting Your Investment Portfolio," we embark on a creative journey through the process of constructing and managing a diversified investment portfolio. Just as a sculptor chisel away at a block of stone to reveal a masterpiece, investors carefully select and shape their investments to achieve their financial goals and withstand the test of time. This chapter delves into the art of portfolio construction, considering asset allocation, risk management, diversification, and the long-term perspective.

1. Understanding Investment Portfolios:

An investment portfolio comprises a collection of assets owned by an individual or institution. We discuss the essence of investment portfolios and their significance in achieving financial objectives.

2. The Art of Asset Allocation:

Asset allocation is the foundation of portfolio construction. We explore the art of allocating investments across different asset classes to optimize risk and return.

3. The Role of Risk Tolerance:

Risk tolerance influences asset allocation decisions. We discuss the art of aligning portfolio risk with individual risk preferences and financial goals.

4. Diversification: The Investor's Chisel:

Diversification reduces risk by spreading investments across different assets. We explore the art of diversification and its importance in mitigating portfolio risk.

5. The Art of Evaluating Risk and Return:

Investors weigh risk and return when selecting assets. We discuss the art of assessing potential risks and expected returns for each investment.

6. The Impact of Investment Time Horizon:

Investment time horizon shapes portfolio construction. We explore the art of tailoring portfolios to short-term, medium-term, and long-term financial goals.

7. The Art of Selecting Investment Vehicles:

Investment vehicles offer different features and risk profiles. We discuss the art of selecting individual stocks, bonds, mutual funds, ETFs, and other investment options.

8. The Role of Active vs. Passive Investing:

Active and passive investment strategies have different approaches. We explore the art of combining active and passive investments to achieve diversified exposure.

9. The Influence of Tax Efficiency:

Tax efficiency is essential in portfolio construction. We discuss the art of minimizing tax implications through strategic asset placement and tax-efficient funds.

10. The Art of Strategic Rebalancing:

Rebalancing involves realigning the portfolio to the target asset allocation. We explore the art of strategic rebalancing to maintain desired risk levels and performance.

11. Building a Solid Core: The Foundation of Your Portfolio:

A core portfolio represents the foundation of an investment strategy. We discuss the art of building a solid core with broad-based index funds or ETFs.

12. The Role of Sector Allocation:

Sector allocation can influence portfolio performance. We explore the art of allocating investments to specific sectors based on market trends and economic conditions.

13. The Art of Sector Rotation:

Sector rotation involves shifting investments based on business cycles. We discuss the art of dynamically adjusting sector allocations for optimal performance.

14. The Impact of Global Diversification:

Global diversification extends investment opportunities. We explore the art of allocating investments across different countries and regions.

15. The Art of Investing in Emerging Markets:

Emerging markets offer growth opportunities but carry higher risks. We discuss the art of investing in emerging markets with a long-term perspective.

16. The Influence of Currency Risk:

Currency risk affects international investments. We explore the art of managing currency risk in a globally diversified portfolio.

17. The Art of Investing in Alternative Assets:

Alternative assets provide portfolio diversification. We discuss the art of incorporating real estate, commodities, hedge funds, and private equity into the portfolio.

18. The Role of Real Assets:

Real assets, such as real estate and infrastructure, offer inflation protection. We explore the art of including real assets in an investment strategy.

19. The Art of Evaluating Investment Fees:

Investment fees impact portfolio returns. We discuss the art of selecting cost-effective investment options to optimize long-term performance.

20. The Future of Portfolio Sculpting:

Portfolio construction techniques will continue to evolve. We speculate on the future of portfolio sculpting, incorporating advancements in technology and investment products.

Conclusion:

"Sculpting Your Investment Portfolio" celebrates the art of constructing a well-balanced and diversified investment masterpiece. Just as a sculptor carefully shapes their work to create a harmonious composition, investors meticulously select and position their assets to achieve their financial aspirations. The art of portfolio construction empowers investors to align their portfolios with their risk preferences, investment time horizon, and long-term goals. As the investment landscape evolves, portfolio sculpting remains a timeless and indispensable approach, guiding investors to build resilient portfolios that endure the challenges of dynamic markets. Through thoughtful portfolio construction, investors can paint a canvas of financial success, blending the stability of core investments with the vibrancy of strategic allocations to create a masterpiece of long-term wealth creation and financial prosperity. Sculpting your investment portfolio becomes the brushstroke that adds depth, resilience, and growth to an investment journey, creating a mosaic of financial security and enduring legacy for generations to come.

CHAPTER 17: THE ARTFUL SCIENCE OF TECHNICAL ANALYSIS

Introduction:

Technical analysis is a fascinating blend of art and science that seeks to interpret and forecast financial markets through the study of historical price and volume data. In Chapter 17, "The Artful Science of Technical Analysis," we embark on a captivating journey through the world of technical analysis, exploring the tools, techniques, and patterns that analysts use to make sense of market behavior. Just as an artist blends colors and textures to create a masterpiece, technical analysts examine charts and patterns to uncover hidden insights and potential investment opportunities. This chapter delves into the art and science of technical analysis, discussing its principles, indicators, and applications.

1. Understanding Technical Analysis:

Technical analysis involves analyzing historical price and volume data to predict future market movements. We discuss the essence of technical analysis and its role in understanding market behavior.

2. The Role of Market Charts:

Market charts are the canvas of technical analysis. We explore the art of reading and interpreting price charts, including line charts, bar charts, and candlestick charts.

3. The Art of Chart Patterns:

Chart patterns are the building blocks of technical analysis. We discuss the art of identifying and analyzing patterns such as head and shoulders, double tops, and triangles.

4. The Influence of Support and Resistance Levels:

Support and resistance levels are critical price levels on charts. We explore the art of recognizing these levels and their significance in market analysis.

5. The Role of Trendlines:

Trendlines help identify market trends and reversals. We discuss the art of drawing trendlines and their importance in technical analysis.

6. The Art of Moving Averages:

Moving averages smooth out price data and reveal trend direction. We explore the art of using simple moving averages (SMA) and exponential moving averages (EMA).

7. The Power of Fibonacci Retracements:

Fibonacci retracements are ratios derived from the Fibonacci sequence. We discuss the art of using Fibonacci levels to identify potential price reversals.

8. The Role of Oscillators:

Oscillators are technical indicators that measure overbought or oversold conditions. We explore the art of using indicators like the Relative Strength Index (RSI) and the Moving Average Convergence Divergence (MACD).

9. The Art of Volume Analysis:

Volume is a crucial component of technical analysis. We discuss the art of analyzing volume to confirm price trends and potential reversals.

10. The Influence of Sentiment Indicators:

Sentiment indicators gauge market sentiment and investor psychology. We explore the art of using indicators like the Put-Call Ratio and the Volatility Index (VIX).

11. The Art of Moving Average Crossovers:

Moving average crossovers signal potential trend changes. We discuss the art of interpreting moving average crossover signals.

12. The Power of Japanese Candlestick Patterns:

Japanese candlestick patterns offer detailed insights into price movements. We explore the art of recognizing patterns like doji, hammer, and engulfing.

13. The Art of Elliott Wave Theory:

Elliott Wave Theory identifies repeating price patterns. We discuss the art of applying wave analysis to forecast market trends.

14. The Impact of Chart Timeframes:

Different chart timeframes offer varying perspectives. We explore the art of using multiple timeframes to gain a comprehensive view of market trends.

15. The Art of Technical Analysis in Trading Strategies:

Technical analysis informs trading strategies. We discuss the art of incorporating technical indicators into trading approaches.

16. The Role of Backtesting:

Backtesting assesses the historical performance of technical strategies. We explore the art of backtesting to validate trading ideas.

17. The Art of Combining Technical and Fundamental Analysis:

Technical and fundamental analysis can complement each other. We discuss the art of integrating technical insights with fundamental research.

18. The Impact of Behavioral Finance on Technical Analysis:

Behavioral biases influence technical analysis. We explore the art of recognizing cognitive biases in market participants and their impact on chart patterns.

19. The Art of Risk Management in Technical Analysis:

Risk management is essential in technical analysis. We discuss the art of setting stop-loss levels and managing risk in trading strategies.

20. The Future of Technical Analysis:

Technical analysis will continue to evolve. We speculate on the future of technical analysis, incorporating technological advancements and new analytical tools.

Conclusion:

"The Artful Science of Technical Analysis" celebrates the captivating blend of art and science that underpins market analysis. Just as an artist carefully observes details and nuances in their work, technical analysts diligently study historical price data to uncover hidden market insights. The art and science of technical analysis empower investors to make well-informed decisions, guided by chart patterns, indicators, and market trends. As the investment landscape evolves, technical analysis remains a timeless and adaptable tool for understanding market behavior and identifying potential trading opportunities. Through the lens of technical analysis, investors can paint a canvas of financial success, blending the creativity of interpretation with the rigor of statistical analysis to create a masterpiece of profitable investment decisions and strategic trading strategies. The artful science of technical analysis becomes the brushstroke that adds depth, precision, and profitability to an investment journey, creating a mosaic of strategic acumen and financial gains that endures the test of time.

CHAPTER 18: GAINING INSIGHTS THROUGH DATA ANALYTICS

Introduction:

Data analytics is a powerful and transformative field that enables investors and businesses to extract valuable insights from vast amounts of data. In Chapter 18, "Gaining Insights through Data Analytics," we embark on a journey through the world of data analytics, exploring the methodologies, tools, and applications that leverage data to make informed decisions. Just as an explorer uncovers hidden treasures in uncharted territories, data analysts delve into the depths of data to reveal valuable patterns and trends. This chapter delves into the art and science of data analytics, discussing its principles, techniques, and the impact it has on investment strategies.

1. Understanding Data Analytics:

Data analytics involves the process of examining, cleaning, transforming, and interpreting data to extract meaningful insights. We discuss the essence of data analytics and its role in gaining a competitive advantage in the investment landscape.

2. The Art of Data Collection and Storage:

Data analytics begins with data collection and storage. We explore the art of acquiring and organizing data from various sources, including financial statements, market data, and alternative data sets.

3. The Role of Big Data and Machine Learning:

Big data and machine learning play a transformative role in data analytics. We discuss the art of leveraging advanced algorithms to process and analyze vast amounts of data.

4. The Power of Data Visualization:

Data visualization is the bridge between data and insights. We explore the art of creating compelling visualizations that facilitate understanding and decision-making.

5. The Influence of Data Cleaning and Preprocessing:

Data quality is crucial for accurate analysis. We discuss the art of cleaning and preprocessing data to remove errors and inconsistencies.

6. The Art of Descriptive Analytics:

Descriptive analytics focuses on understanding historical data patterns. We explore the art of summarizing and visualizing past data to gain insights into past market behavior.

7. The Role of Predictive Analytics:

Predictive analytics forecasts future trends and outcomes. We discuss the art of using statistical models and machine learning algorithms to make data-driven predictions.

8. The Power of Sentiment Analysis:

Sentiment analysis measures public sentiment about companies, stocks, or the market. We explore the art of using natural language processing (NLP) to analyze sentiment from news articles, social media, and other sources.

9. The Art of Exploratory Data Analysis (EDA):

EDA involves interactive data exploration to uncover patterns and relationships. We discuss the art of using EDA techniques to discover insights in raw data.

10. The Influence of Quantitative Analysis:

Quantitative analysis involves applying mathematical and statistical techniques to data. We explore the art of using quantitative models to make investment decisions.

11. The Art of Correlation and Regression Analysis:

Correlation and regression analyze relationships between variables. We discuss the art of measuring correlations and using regression to predict future outcomes.

12. The Role of Time Series Analysis:

Time series analysis examines data collected over time. We explore the art of forecasting trends and identifying seasonality in financial data.

13. The Art of Data Mining:

Data mining uncovers patterns and relationships in large datasets. We discuss the art of using data mining techniques to find investment opportunities.

14. The Power of Risk Analytics:

Risk analytics assesses and manages portfolio risk. We explore the art of using risk models to optimize risk-adjusted returns.

15. The Influence of Algorithmic Trading and Quantitative Strategies:

Algorithmic trading relies on data analytics for decision-making. We discuss the art of incorporating data analytics into quantitative trading strategies.

16. The Art of Backtesting and Performance Evaluation:

Backtesting assesses the performance of trading strategies using historical data. We explore the art of evaluating strategy effectiveness and making improvements based on data insights.

17. The Role of Data Ethics and Privacy:

Data analytics raises ethical and privacy concerns. We discuss the art of handling data responsibly and protecting sensitive information.

18. The Art of Applying Data Analytics in ESG Investing:

Data analytics supports ESG (Environmental, Social, and Governance) investing. We explore the art of using data insights to make sustainable investment decisions.

19. The Influence of Data-Driven Decision-Making in Portfolio Management:

Data-driven decision-making enhances portfolio management. We discuss the art of integrating data analytics into investment processes.

20. The Future of Data Analytics:

Data analytics will continue to evolve with technological advancements. We speculate on the future of data analytics, incorporating AI, advanced algorithms, and real-time data processing.

Conclusion:

"Gaining Insights through Data Analytics" celebrates the transformative power of data analytics in the investment landscape. Just as an explorer uncovers hidden treasures through exploration, data analysts unearth valuable insights from vast data sets. The art and science of data analytics empower investors to make informed decisions, guided by patterns, trends, and correlations revealed in data. As the investment landscape evolves, data analytics remains a timeless and indispensable tool for gaining a competitive edge and making data-driven investment decisions. Through the lens of data analytics, investors can paint a canvas of financial success, blending the creativity of exploration with the rigor of statistical analysis to create a masterpiece of profitable investment strategies and informed decision-making. Gaining insights through data analytics becomes the brushstroke that adds depth, precision, and strategic acumen to an investment journey, creating a mosaic of data-driven intelligence and enduring financial prosperity for generations to come.

CHAPTER 19: ARTISTIC INSIGHTS FROM LEGENDARY INVESTORS

Introduction:

Legendary investors are like master artists, creating their financial masterpieces with wisdom, experience, and a unique perspective. In Chapter 19, "Artistic Insights from Legendary Investors," we delve into the teachings and philosophies of some of the most celebrated investors in history. Just as an artist leaves a lasting impact with their creative genius, legendary investors have shaped the world of finance with their remarkable insights and successful strategies. This chapter explores the artistic brilliance of legendary investors, examining their investment principles, philosophies, and the timeless lessons they impart to aspiring investors.

1. The Art of Value Investing: Warren Buffett

Warren Buffett, often regarded as the Oracle of Omaha, epitomizes the art of value investing. We explore Buffett's timeless principles, including the importance of a long-term perspective, investing in quality businesses, and seeking a margin of safety.

2. The Influence of Growth Investing: Peter Lynch

Peter Lynch, renowned for his exceptional track record as a growth investor, provides artistic insights into identifying promising growth stocks. We discuss Lynch's "buy what you know" philosophy and the art of spotting emerging trends.

3. The Art of Contrarian Investing: Sir John Templeton

Sir John Templeton, a pioneer of global investing, offers artistic insights into contrarian thinking. We explore Templeton's emphasis on seeking opportunities where others fear to tread and his unwavering optimism in times of uncertainty.

4. The Wisdom of Benjamin Graham: The Father of Value Investing

Benjamin Graham, the father of value investing, left a profound impact on the investment world. We discuss Graham's emphasis on fundamental analysis, the margin of safety, and the art of preserving capital.

5. The Art of Risk Management: Ray Dalio

Ray Dalio, founder of Bridgewater Associates, emphasizes the importance of risk management in investment strategies. We explore Dalio's principles, including "radical transparency" and the art of learning from mistakes.

6. The Impact of Technical Analysis: John J. Murphy

John J. Murphy, a legendary technical analyst, provides artistic insights into reading market charts. We discuss Murphy's principles of trend analysis, support and resistance, and the art of understanding market psychology.

7. The Art of Macro Investing: George Soros

George Soros, a master of macro investing, offers artistic insights into understanding the broader economic and political landscape. We explore Soros's philosophy of reflexivity and the art of identifying turning points in financial markets.

8. The Art of Hedge Fund Management: David Einhorn

David Einhorn, a prominent hedge fund manager, shares artistic insights into his investment approach. We discuss Einhorn's focus on value investing, short selling, and the art of expressing contrarian views.

9. The Influence of Global Macro Investing: Stanley Druckenmiller

Stanley Druckenmiller, a legendary macro investor, offers

artistic insights into navigating global markets. We explore Druckenmiller's principles of risk management, flexibility, and the art of capitalizing on market trends.

10. The Art of Distressed Investing: Howard Marks

Howard Marks, known for his expertise in distressed investing, imparts artistic insights into investing in distressed assets. We discuss Marks's philosophy of contrarian thinking, risk control, and the art of identifying value in troubled assets.

11. The Wisdom of Charlie Munger: The Artistic Partner of Warren Buffett

Charlie Munger, Warren Buffett's longtime business partner, offers a wealth of artistic insights into investment and life. We explore Munger's principles, including the importance of mental models, lifelong learning, and the art of decision-making.

12. The Art of Concentrated Investing: Bill Ackman

Bill Ackman, a prominent activist investor, provides artistic insights into concentrated investing. We discuss Ackman's philosophy of in-depth research, conviction, and the art of capitalizing on undervalued opportunities.

13. The Impact of Global Value Investing: Sir Christopher Hohn

Sir Christopher Hohn, a leading global value investor, offers artistic insights into his investment approach. We explore Hohn's principles of long-term value investing, shareholder activism, and the art of pursuing sustainable change.

14. The Art of ESG Investing: Jeremy Grantham

Jeremy Grantham, a seasoned investor and advocate for environmental, social, and governance (ESG) investing, shares artistic insights into sustainable investing. We discuss Grantham's principles of responsible investing and the art of aligning investments with positive societal impact.

15. The Wisdom of Sir James Goldsmith: The Artistic

Financier

Sir James Goldsmith, a renowned financier and corporate raider, imparts artistic insights into his unique investment philosophy. We explore Goldsmith's principles, including skepticism towards conventional wisdom and the art of questioning prevailing assumptions.

16. The Art of Philanthropic Investing: George Soros

George Soros, beyond his investment success, is known for his philanthropic endeavors. We discuss the art of philanthropic investing, leveraging wealth for societal good, and the power of the "Open Society" philosophy.

17. The Art of Emotional Intelligence in Investing: Daniel Kahneman

Daniel Kahneman, a Nobel laureate in economics, provides artistic insights into the role of emotions in decision-making. We explore Kahneman's principles of behavioral finance, cognitive biases, and the art of self-awareness in investment choices.

18. The Influence of Long-Term Thinking: Pat Dorsey

Pat Dorsey, a seasoned investor and author, offers artistic insights into long-term investing. We discuss Dorsey's focus on durable competitive advantages and the art of building robust investment theses.

19. The Art of Investment Philosophy: Joel Greenblatt

Joel Greenblatt, known for his "Magic Formula" approach to investing, provides artistic insights into the importance of having a clear investment philosophy. We explore Greenblatt's principles of simplicity, value-based investing, and the art of focusing on factors that drive investment returns.

20. The Wisdom of Philip Fisher: The Artistic Growth Investor

Philip Fisher, a pioneer of growth investing, offers artistic insights into his approach to identifying growth stocks. We discuss Fisher's focus on in-depth research, understanding a company's competitive advantage, and the art of investing with a long-term horizon.

21. The Art of Geopolitical Investing: Felix Zulauf

Felix Zulauf, a renowned geopolitical investor, imparts artistic insights into the impact of geopolitical events on financial markets. We explore Zulauf's principles of understanding global trends, the art of assessing political risks, and the importance of adaptability.

22. The Influence of Deep Value Investing: Seth Klarman

Seth Klarman, a highly respected value investor, provides artistic insights into deep value investing. We discuss Klarman's principles of margin of safety, contrarian thinking, and the art of capitalizing on market inefficiencies.

23. The Art of Tactical Asset Allocation: Gary Shilling

Gary Shilling, a prominent economist and investor, offers artistic insights into tactical asset allocation. We explore Shilling's principles of macroeconomic analysis, risk management, and the art of positioning investments based on economic trends.

24. The Wisdom of Louise Yamada: The Artistic Technical Analyst

Louise Yamada, a trailblazing technical analyst, shares artistic insights into the world of technical analysis. We discuss Yamada's principles of chart patterns, trend analysis, and the art of interpreting market behavior through charts.

25. The Art of Bottom-Up Investing: Mario Gabelli

Mario Gabelli, a master of bottom-up investing, provides artistic insights into his investment philosophy. We explore Gabelli's focus on individual stock analysis, the art of identifying undervalued opportunities, and the importance of a strong research process.

26. The Influence of Quantitative Analysis: Cliff Asness

Cliff Asness, a prominent quantitative investor, offers artistic insights into the world of quantitative finance. We discuss Asness's principles of factor investing, risk premiums, and the art of combining quantitative and fundamental analysis.

27. The Art of Index Investing: John C. Bogle

John C. Bogle, the founder of Vanguard and a pioneer of index investing, imparts artistic insights into the power of passive investing. We explore Bogle's principles of low-cost investing, diversification, and the art of achieving market returns with simplicity.

28. The Wisdom of Charles Munger: The Artistic Partner of Warren Buffett

Charles Munger, Warren Buffett's longtime business partner, provides artistic insights into a wide range of disciplines, including investing. We discuss Munger's principles of multidisciplinary thinking, mental models, and the art of making rational decisions.

29. The Art of Arbitrage Investing: Bruce Greenwald

Bruce Greenwald, an expert in value investing and arbitrage, offers artistic insights into the world of arbitrage investing. We explore Greenwald's principles of identifying mispriced assets, risk management, and the art of capturing market inefficiencies.

30. The Influence of Quantitative Macro Investing: Ray Dalio

Ray Dalio, beyond his expertise in risk management, provides artistic insights into quantitative macro investing. We discuss Dalio's principles of economic indicators, currency analysis, and the art of understanding the global economic landscape.

Conclusion:

"Artistic Insights from Legendary Investors" celebrates the

wisdom and ingenuity of the investment masters who have left an indelible mark on the financial world. Just as master artists leave a legacy of timeless creations, legendary investors impart valuable insights and philosophies that continue to inspire and guide investors worldwide. The artistic brilliance of these investors lies not only in their success but also in the principles they espouse - from value investing and growth investing to technical analysis and risk management.

As the investment landscape continues to evolve, the artistic insights from legendary investors remain a treasure trove of wisdom for both seasoned investors and aspiring novices. Embracing the artistic insights of these investment gurus empowers investors to develop their own unique style and approach, combining the rigor of analysis with the intuition of experience to create a masterpiece of profitable investment strategies and resilient financial decision-making.

Through the lens of artistic insights from legendary investors, investors can paint a canvas of financial success, blending the wisdom of the past with the innovation of the present to create a mosaic of strategic acumen and enduring financial prosperity. "Artistic Insights from Legendary Investors" becomes the brushstroke that adds depth, vision, and profitability to an investment journey, creating a legacy of inspired investment decisions and the pursuit of excellence for generations to come.

CHAPTER 20: INVESTING IN GLOBAL MASTERPIECES

Introduction:

Investing in global masterpieces represents a unique and fascinating intersection between the worlds of art and finance. In Chapter 20, "Investing in Global Masterpieces," we embark on a captivating journey through the realm of art investment, exploring the allure of investing in valuable artworks and the factors that make them coveted masterpieces. Just as an art collector carefully curates their collection, investors seek to acquire and own exceptional artworks that not only appreciate in value but also bring cultural significance. This chapter delves into the art and science of art investment, discussing the principles of art valuation, market trends, and the impact of art as an alternative investment asset.

1. Understanding Art as an Investment:

Art as an investment involves acquiring valuable artworks with the expectation of appreciation over time. We discuss the essence of art investment and its role in diversifying investment portfolios.

2. The Art Market Ecosystem:

The art market has a unique ecosystem comprising artists, galleries, auction houses, and collectors. We explore the art market's structure and the key players that drive art prices.

3. The Role of Art Valuation:

Art valuation is a complex process that determines an artwork's worth. We discuss the art of valuing artworks based on artist reputation, provenance, condition, and historical significance.

4. The Influence of Art Movements and Styles:

Art movements and styles impact an artwork's value and demand. We explore the art of understanding different art movements, from Renaissance to Contemporary art.

5. The Art of Building an Art Collection:

Art collectors create curated collections that reflect their tastes and interests. We discuss the art of building an art collection with a focus on aesthetics, cultural significance, and potential investment returns.

6. The Power of Blue-Chip Artists:

Blue-chip artists are established and highly sought-after in the art market. We explore the art of investing in artworks by renowned artists like Picasso, Monet, and Warhol.

7. The Role of Emerging Artists:

Emerging artists offer potential for significant returns. We discuss the art of identifying talented emerging artists and investing in their early works.

8. The Art of Art Investment Funds:

Art investment funds pool investor capital to acquire art. We explore the art of investing in art funds and the potential benefits of diversification.

9. The Influence of Art as a Safe Haven:

Art is often considered a safe haven asset during economic uncertainties. We discuss the art of using art as a hedge against inflation and market volatility.

10. The Art Market's Global Dynamics:

The art market operates on a global scale, with buyers and sellers from different countries. We explore the art of navigating the global art market and the impact of cultural differences on art values.

11. The Role of Auction Houses:

Auction houses play a pivotal role in art sales. We discuss the art of buying and selling artworks through major auction houses like Christie's and Sotheby's.

12. The Art of Art Investment Research:

Research is vital in making informed art investment decisions. We explore the art of conducting due diligence on artworks, artists, and market trends.

13. The Power of Art Indices:

Art indices track the performance of the art market. We discuss the art of using art indices for performance comparison and benchmarking.

14. The Art of Art Investment Appraisal:

Art investment appraisal involves periodic evaluation of art holdings. We explore the art of assessing the value and performance of an art portfolio.

15. The Influence of Art Market Liquidity:

Art market liquidity can impact buying and selling decisions. We discuss the art of understanding liquidity and the implications for art investment strategies.

16. The Art of Art Storage and Conservation:

Art storage and conservation are crucial for preserving an artwork's value. We explore the art of maintaining artworks in optimal conditions.

17. The Role of Art Investment Advisory:

Art investment advisors provide specialized guidance to art investors. We discuss the art of selecting reliable art advisors and the benefits of professional advice.

18. The Art of Investing in Art Funds:

Art funds offer diversified exposure to artworks. We explore the art of investing in art funds and the potential risks and rewards.

19. The Impact of Art Authentication:

Art authentication verifies the authenticity of artworks. We discuss the art of navigating the authentication process and its influence on art value.

20. The Art of Art Insurance:

Art insurance protects against loss or damage to artworks. We explore the art of obtaining comprehensive art insurance coverage.

21. The Future of Art Investment:

Art investment will continue to evolve with changing market dynamics. We speculate on the future of art investment, incorporating technological advancements and shifting collector preferences.

Conclusion:

In conclusion, "Investing in Global Masterpieces" celebrates the unique and alluring world of art investment, where the aesthetic beauty of masterpieces converges with the potential for financial appreciation and cultural significance. Just as an art collector curates a collection with passion and discernment, art investors have the opportunity to build portfolios that transcend monetary value, becoming a reflection of cultural heritage and artistic expression. By embracing the art and science of art investment, investors can paint a canvas of financial success, combining the creativity of the art world with the strategic acumen of investment analysis, creating a masterpiece of diverse, culturally significant, and financially rewarding investment holdings that endure the test of time. Investing in global masterpieces becomes the brushstroke that adds depth, beauty, and profound value to an investment journey, creating a legacy of inspired investment decisions and cultural preservation for generations to come.

CHAPTER 21: THE EMOTIONAL PALETTE: MANAGING INVESTMENT PSYCHOLOGY

Introduction:

Investing is not merely a numbers game; it is also a psychological journey. In Chapter 21, "The Emotional Palette: Managing Investment Psychology," we delve into the fascinating world of investment psychology, exploring the powerful impact emotions have on investment decisions. Just as an artist skillfully blends colors to create a masterpiece, successful investors manage their emotional palette to make rational, disciplined, and successful choices. This chapter examines the intricate interplay of emotions and investment behavior, discussing the common psychological biases, techniques for managing emotions, and the art of cultivating a resilient investment mindset.

1. The Psychology of Investing:

Investment psychology involves understanding how human emotions influence decision-making in the financial markets. We discuss the essence of investment psychology and its significance in shaping investment outcomes.

2. The Role of Behavioral Finance:

Behavioral finance studies how cognitive biases affect financial decisions. We explore the art of recognizing common biases, such as loss aversion and overconfidence, and their impact on investment behavior.

3. The Art of Self-Awareness:

Self-awareness is the foundation of managing investment

psychology. We discuss the art of introspection, recognizing one's emotional triggers, and understanding personal risk tolerance.

4. The Influence of Fear and Greed:

Fear and greed are powerful emotions that drive market sentiment. We explore the art of managing fear during market downturns and tempering greed during periods of exuberance.

5. The Art of Decision-Making:

Investment decisions are influenced by cognitive biases and emotions. We discuss the art of making rational decisions, embracing uncertainty, and the role of intuition in investment choices.

6. The Power of Patience:

Patience is a virtue in investing. We explore the art of cultivating patience, resisting impulsive actions, and appreciating the value of long-term investment horizons.

7. The Role of Mental Accounting:

Mental accounting affects how investors perceive gains and losses. We discuss the art of rationalizing investment decisions and treating each investment as part of a cohesive portfolio.

8. The Art of Loss Aversion:

Loss aversion leads investors to avoid realizing losses. We explore the art of managing loss aversion, setting stop-loss levels, and recognizing when to cut losses.

9. The Impact of Herding Behavior:

Herding behavior influences market trends. We discuss the art of avoiding herd mentality, conducting independent research, and maintaining a contrarian perspective.

10. The Art of Investment Discipline:

Investment discipline is crucial for successful outcomes. We explore the art of sticking to an investment strategy, avoiding emotional trading, and maintaining a long-term focus.

11. The Role of Regret Aversion:

Regret aversion hinders decision-making. We discuss the art of learning from mistakes, accepting losses, and using regrets as lessons for future improvements.

12. The Art of Visualization:

Visualization can enhance investment performance. We explore the art of visualizing investment goals, envisioning success, and staying motivated during challenging times.

13. The Power of Emotional Resilience:

Emotional resilience is key to navigating market volatility. We discuss the art of bouncing back from setbacks, staying optimistic, and maintaining composure during market turbulence.

14. The Art of Mindfulness:

Mindfulness enhances decision-making and reduces stress. We explore the art of practicing mindfulness, staying present in the moment, and detaching from emotional reactions.

15. The Influence of Confirmation Bias:

Confirmation bias reinforces pre-existing beliefs. We discuss the art of seeking diverse viewpoints, challenging assumptions, and avoiding tunnel vision in investment analysis.

16. The Art of Goal Setting:

Clear goals drive investment discipline. We explore the art of setting SMART (Specific, Measurable, Achievable, Relevant, Time-bound) investment goals and tracking progress.

17. The Role of Financial Education:

Financial education fosters confident decision-making. We discuss the art of continuous learning, improving financial literacy, and seeking expert advice when needed.

18. The Art of Coping with Market Uncertainty:

Market uncertainty is inevitable. We explore the art of embracing uncertainty, maintaining a diversified portfolio, and adapting investment strategies as conditions change.

19. The Power of Gratitude:

Gratitude enhances overall well-being, including investment mindset. We discuss the art of practicing gratitude, appreciating gains, and maintaining perspective during losses.

20. The Art of Positive Reinforcement:

Positive reinforcement fosters disciplined behavior. We explore the art of rewarding investment milestones, celebrating successes, and using positive reinforcement to stay motivated.

21. The Influence of Cognitive Flexibility:

Cognitive flexibility enhances adaptability. We discuss the art of being open to new information, revising investment strategies when necessary, and learning from market shifts.

Conclusion:

"The Emotional Palette: Managing Investment Psychology" celebrates the intricate relationship between emotions and investment behavior. Just as an artist balances colors and emotions to create a harmonious painting, successful investors manage their emotional palette to make informed, rational decisions that align with their long-term goals. The art and science of managing investment psychology empower investors to become masters of their emotions, cultivating self-awareness, discipline, and resilience.

As the investment landscape continues to present challenges and opportunities, understanding investment psychology becomes an essential tool for thriving in the markets. By embracing the art of managing emotions and the science of behavioral finance, investors can paint a canvas of financial success, blending the emotional intelligence of self-awareness with the analytical rigor of rational decision-making. "The Emotional Palette: Managing Investment Psychology" becomes the brushstroke that adds depth, wisdom, and profitability to an investment journey, creating a legacy of empowered investors who navigate market fluctuations with confidence and grace. In the tapestry of investment success, the management of investment psychology becomes the masterpiece, reflecting the fusion of emotional intelligence and strategic acumen that endures the test of time.

CHAPTER 22: ARTFUL ALCHEMY: TRANSFORMING RISK INTO REWARD

Introduction:

Investing is inherently linked to risk, but successful investors possess the artful ability to transform risk into reward. In Chapter 22, "Artful Alchemy: Transforming Risk into Reward," we embark on a captivating journey through the world of investment risk, exploring the art and science of managing risk to achieve desirable investment outcomes. Just as an alchemist seeks to turn base metals into gold, investors aim to optimize risk-taking to maximize returns. This chapter delves into the various dimensions of risk, risk management strategies, and the art of finding the delicate balance between risk and reward in pursuit of financial success.

1. Understanding Investment Risk:

Investment risk encompasses the potential for losses or deviations from expected returns. We discuss the essence of investment risk and its integral role in investment decision-making.

2. The Art of Risk Appetite:

Risk appetite varies among investors and influences their investment strategies. We explore the art of determining risk appetite, aligning it with financial goals, and embracing risk as an opportunity.

3. The Influence of Risk Tolerance:

Risk tolerance reflects an investor's ability to withstand market fluctuations. We discuss the art of assessing risk tolerance, maintaining composure during market turbulence, and avoiding emotional decision-making.

4. The Art of Diversification:

Diversification is a powerful risk management tool. We explore the art of building diversified portfolios, spreading risk across different asset classes, industries, and geographic regions.

5. The Power of Asset Allocation:

Asset allocation drives investment returns and risk exposure. We discuss the art of strategic asset allocation, balancing risk and reward through a well-thought-out allocation strategy.

6. The Role of Risk-Adjusted Return:

Risk-adjusted return measures an investment's performance relative to its risk. We explore the art of optimizing risk-adjusted returns and identifying investments with favorable risk-reward profiles.

7. The Art of Due Diligence:

Thorough due diligence minimizes investment risk. We discuss the art of researching investment opportunities, analyzing financial statements, and evaluating the quality of assets.

8. The Influence of Systemic Risk:

Systemic risk affects the entire financial system. We explore the art of understanding and mitigating systemic risk through portfolio diversification and risk monitoring.

9. The Art of Contingency Planning:

Contingency planning prepares investors for unforeseen events. We discuss the art of having contingency plans in place to address adverse market conditions.

10. The Power of Risk Management Techniques:

Risk management techniques protect against potential losses. We explore the art of using stop-loss orders, hedging strategies, and other risk management tools.

11. The Art of Stress Testing:

Stress testing assesses portfolio resilience under extreme scenarios. We discuss the art of stress testing investments to prepare for worst-case scenarios.

12. The Influence of Behavioral Risk:

Behavioral risk arises from cognitive biases and emotional decision-making. We explore the art of recognizing and mitigating behavioral risk to make rational investment choices.

13. The Art of Risk-Return Tradeoff:

The risk-return tradeoff governs investment decisions. We discuss the art of seeking an optimal balance between risk and return, considering an investment's potential upside and downside.

14. The Role of Risk Budgeting:

Risk budgeting allocates risk to different components of a portfolio. We explore the art of risk budgeting, aligning risk exposure with investment objectives and constraints.

15. The Art of Selecting Risk Factors:

Factor investing involves targeting specific risk factors for higher returns. We discuss the art of identifying and selecting risk factors that align with investment goals.

16. The Power of Risk Monitoring:

Continuous risk monitoring ensures the portfolio stays aligned with objectives. We explore the art of regularly evaluating risk exposures and making adjustments as needed.

17. The Art of Crisis Management:

Crisis management involves navigating market downturns and black swan events. We discuss the art of staying calm under pressure, identifying opportunities in crises, and avoiding panic-driven actions.

18. The Influence of Liquidity Risk:

Liquidity risk affects the ability to buy or sell assets at fair prices. We explore the art of managing liquidity risk, considering investment horizons and market conditions.

19. The Art of Volatility Management:

Volatility management mitigates the impact of market fluctuations. We discuss the art of using volatility-based strategies, such as options, to manage risk exposure.

20. The Role of Risk Communication:

Effective risk communication fosters investor confidence. We explore the art of transparently communicating risk to stakeholders and managing expectations.

21. The Art of Risk Assessment:

Risk assessment involves quantifying potential risks and their impact. We discuss the art of conducting risk assessments, scenario planning, and stress testing.

22. The Influence of Environmental, Social, and Governance (ESG) Risks:

ESG risks impact investment sustainability and reputation. We explore the art of integrating ESG considerations into investment analysis and decision-making.

Conclusion:

"Artful Alchemy: Transforming Risk into Reward" celebrates the mastery of turning investment risk into profitable rewards. Just as an alchemist seeks to unlock the secrets of transmutation, successful investors possess the artful ability to optimize risk-taking and leverage it to their advantage. The art and science of managing investment risk empower investors to create portfolios that balance potential rewards with prudent risk management.

As the investment landscape evolves, understanding risk and its transformation into reward becomes an essential tool for thriving in dynamic markets. By embracing the art of risk management and the science of portfolio optimization, investors can paint a canvas of financial success, combining the creativity of calculated risk-taking with the analytical rigor of investment analysis. "Artful Alchemy: Transforming Risk into Reward" becomes the brushstroke that adds depth, wisdom, and profitability to an investment journey, creating a legacy of empowered investors who navigate market fluctuations with confidence and grace. In the tapestry of investment success, the management of risk becomes the masterpiece, reflecting the fusion of analytical acumen, emotional intelligence, and strategic thinking. By embracing the artful alchemy of transforming risk into reward, investors can overcome the inherent challenges of investing, seize opportunities amid market fluctuations, and consistently achieve financial prosperity.

CHAPTER 23: THE GALLERY OF ALTERNATIVE INVESTMENTS

Introduction:

In Chapter 23, "The Gallery of Alternative Investments," we embark on a captivating journey through the diverse and intriguing world of alternative investments. Just as an art gallery showcases a wide range of artistic masterpieces, the gallery of alternative investments presents a collection of non-traditional assets that offer unique opportunities for investors seeking to diversify their portfolios. This chapter explores the art and science of alternative investments, discussing the various types of alternatives, their benefits, risks, and the art of incorporating them into a well-rounded investment strategy.

1. Understanding Alternative Investments:

Alternative investments refer to assets beyond traditional stocks, bonds, and cash. We discuss the essence of alternative investments and their role in providing diversification and potential for enhanced returns.

2. The Art of Portfolio Diversification:

Diversification is a fundamental principle of investing. We explore the art of using alternative investments to diversify portfolios and reduce overall risk.

3. The Influence of Real Estate Investment:

Real estate is a tangible and popular alternative investment. We discuss the art of investing in residential, commercial, and real estate investment trusts (REITs).

4. The Power of Private Equity:

Private equity offers opportunities to invest in privately-held companies. We explore the art of private equity investments, including venture capital and buyout funds.

5. The Art of Hedge Funds:

Hedge funds are actively managed investment funds. We discuss the art of investing in hedge funds, including long-short equity, event-driven, and global macro strategies.

6. The Role of Commodities:

Commodities provide exposure to physical assets like gold, oil, and agricultural products. We explore the art of investing in commodities and their role as a hedge against inflation.

7. The Art of Venture Capital:

Venture capital supports early-stage companies with high growth potential. We discuss the art of venture capital investing, including evaluating start-up opportunities and managing risk.

8. The Influence of Private Debt:

Private debt involves lending to non-public companies. We explore the art of investing in private debt funds and understanding credit risk.

9. The Power of Infrastructure Investments:

Infrastructure investments include assets like toll roads, airports, and renewable energy projects. We discuss the art of infrastructure investing and its potential for stable returns.

10. The Art of Art and Collectibles:

Art and collectibles offer a unique blend of passion and investment potential. We explore the art of investing in fine art, rare coins, stamps, and other collectible assets.

11. The Role of Cryptocurrencies:

Cryptocurrencies, led by Bitcoin and Ethereum, have gained prominence as alternative digital assets. We discuss the art of investing in cryptocurrencies and understanding their unique risks.

12. The Art of Timberland Investments:

Timberland investments involve owning and managing forested land. We explore the art of timberland investing and its appeal as a renewable resource.

13. The Influence of Structured Products:

Structured products offer customized investment solutions. We discuss the art of understanding structured notes, equity-linked investments, and principal-protected products.

14. The Power of Farmland Investments:

Farmland investments involve agricultural land acquisitions. We explore the art of investing in farmland and its role in food security and sustainable agriculture.

15. The Art of Peer-to-Peer Lending:

Peer-to-peer lending platforms facilitate direct lending between individuals and businesses. We discuss the art of peer-to-peer lending as an alternative fixed-income investment.

16. The Role of Distressed Assets:

Distressed assets present opportunities for value investors. We explore the art of investing in distressed debt, real estate, and other assets with recovery potential.

17. The Art of Royalty-Based Investments:

Royalty-based investments involve purchasing future royalties from creative works. We discuss the art of royalty investing in music, films, and intellectual property.

18. The Influence of Social Impact Investing:

Social impact investing combines financial returns with positive social and environmental outcomes. We explore the art of aligning investments with values and societal impact.

19. The Power of Fine Wine and Spirits:

Fine wine and spirits offer potential for appreciation and collectability. We discuss the art of investing in rare wines and aged spirits.

20. The Art of Vintage Cars and Luxury Assets:

Vintage cars and luxury assets appeal to collectors and investors alike. We explore the art of investing in classic cars, luxury watches, and rare jewelry.

21. The Role of Catastrophe Bonds:

Catastrophe bonds provide insurance against natural disasters. We discuss the art of investing in cat bonds and understanding catastrophe risk.

22. The Art of Investing in Sports:

Sports investments include teams, franchises, and sports-related businesses. We explore the art of sports investing and its intersection with entertainment and media.

23. The Influence of Artificial Intelligence and Robotics:

Artificial intelligence (AI) and robotics present opportunities in technological advancement. We discuss the art of investing in AI, robotics, and automation.

24. The Power of Water and Natural Resources:

Water and natural resource investments have strategic importance. We explore the art of investing in water infrastructure, mining, and renewable energy.

25. The Art of Collectivized Investment:

Collectivized investment platforms enable fractional ownership of assets. We discuss the art of investing in real estate crowdfunding and digital assets.

26. The Role of Global Macro Strategies:

Global macro strategies capitalize on global economic trends. We explore the art of global macro investing and understanding macroeconomic indicators.

27. The Art of Multi-Strategy Hedge Funds:

Multi-strategy hedge funds employ diverse investment approaches. We discuss the art of investing in multi-strategy funds and the benefits of flexible asset allocation.

28. The Influence of Insurance-Linked Securities:

Insurance-linked securities offer risk transfer solutions. We explore the art of investing in catastrophe bonds and reinsurance-linked assets.

29. The Power of Business Development Companies:

Business Development Companies (BDCs) provide financing to small and medium-sized businesses. We discuss the art of investing in BDCs and understanding credit risk.

30. The Art of Short Selling:

Short selling allows investors to profit from declining asset prices. We explore the art of short selling as a hedging and speculative strategy.

Conclusion:

"The Gallery of Alternative Investments" celebrates the rich diversity of non-traditional assets available to investors, akin to a gallery showcasing a wide array of artistic masterpieces. These alternative investments offer a mosaic of opportunities for those seeking to diversify their portfolios beyond conventional stocks and bonds, and each asset type brings its own unique characteristics, risks, and rewards.

Incorporating alternative investments into a well-rounded portfolio provides numerous benefits. The art of portfolio diversification is enhanced through exposure to assets that exhibit low correlation to traditional markets. By diversifying across different asset classes and strategies, investors can reduce overall portfolio risk and improve the potential for more stable returns, especially during times of market turbulence.

Real estate, with its tangible nature and potential for income generation, serves as a solid foundation in the gallery of alternative investments. Investing in residential or commercial properties, or participating in Real Estate Investment Trusts (REITs), allows investors to tap into the wealth-building potential of the real estate market.

Private equity adds a touch of exclusivity to the gallery, offering opportunities to invest in promising startups or established private companies with high growth potential. Venture capital, a subset of private equity, provides early-stage funding to innovative businesses, allowing investors to participate in the dynamic world of entrepreneurship.

Hedge funds, with their actively managed strategies, contribute a sense of artful sophistication to the gallery. Hedge funds employ diverse investment approaches, aiming to generate positive returns in both rising and falling markets, offering investors unique strategies to navigate various market conditions.

Commodities, with their physicality and role as essential resources, provide an essential hue to the gallery of alternative investments. Investing in precious metals, agricultural products, or energy resources offers diversification benefits and serves as a hedge against inflation.

Cryptocurrencies add a touch of modernity and innovation to the gallery, representing a new frontier of digital assets. Bitcoin and other cryptocurrencies have emerged as alternative stores of value and means of exchange, capturing the attention of both traditional and new-age investors.

Private debt investments, farmland, infrastructure, and timberland add a sense of sustainability and stability to the gallery, as they often offer consistent cash flows and potential appreciation over time. These assets play a crucial role in supporting essential sectors and addressing global challenges.

Art and collectibles, with their allure and emotional appeal, infuse the gallery with a sense of passion and cultural significance. Investing in fine art, rare coins, and other collectible assets allows investors to combine their love for aesthetics with the potential for financial appreciation.

Social impact investing showcases the power of aligning investment goals with positive societal and environmental outcomes. Investors who embrace social impact investing aim to make a positive difference while generating financial returns.

Each alternative investment on display in the gallery comes with its own set of risks and complexities. The art of alternative investing involves thorough research, due diligence, and a keen understanding of each asset's unique characteristics.

As the investment landscape continues to evolve, the gallery of alternative investments will undoubtedly welcome new additions, reflecting the dynamic nature of financial markets. As investors explore these diverse opportunities, they must remember that a carefully curated gallery of alternative investments can play a pivotal role in building resilient portfolios that stand the test of time and offer the potential for achieving both financial success and personal fulfillment.

"The Gallery of Alternative Investments" celebrates the confluence of creativity, innovation, and prudence in the pursuit of diversified and rewarding investment portfolios. Just as an art enthusiast carefully curates a gallery of masterpieces, investors can skillfully assemble a gallery of alternative investments that reflects their individual preferences, financial goals, and risk appetite. By embracing the art and science of alternative investing, investors can paint a canvas of financial success, combining the allure of unique investment opportunities with the analytical rigor of portfolio optimization. The gallery of alternative investments becomes the brushstroke that adds depth, diversity, and value to an investment journey, creating a legacy of empowered investors who navigate the complexities of modern finance with confidence and foresight. In the tapestry of investment success, the gallery of alternative investments becomes the masterpiece, reflecting the fusion of vision, strategy, and adaptability that endures the test of time.

CHAPTER 24: BUILDING A MASTERPIECE: CREATING A LONG-TERM PLAN

Introduction:

In Chapter 24, "Building a Masterpiece: Creating a Long-Term Plan," we embark on a comprehensive journey through the process of crafting a strategic and robust long-term investment plan. Just as a master artist carefully plans each stroke on the canvas, successful investors must design a well-thought-out plan to achieve their financial objectives. This chapter delves into the art and science of long-term planning, discussing the key elements of a financial plan, goal setting, risk assessment, asset allocation, and the importance of periodic review and adjustments to ensure the plan remains on track.

1. The Foundation of Long-Term Planning:

Long-term planning serves as the bedrock of successful investing. We discuss the essence of a long-term perspective and the benefits of aligning investments with financial goals.

2. The Art of Goal Setting:

Goal setting is the cornerstone of a long-term plan. We explore the art of defining clear and achievable financial goals, such as retirement, education funding, and wealth accumulation.

3. The Power of Time Horizons:

Time horizons shape investment strategies. We discuss the art of considering different time frames for each financial goal and adjusting risk profiles accordingly.

4. The Art of Risk Assessment:

Risk assessment is crucial for prudent planning. We explore the art of evaluating risk tolerance, understanding risk capacity, and incorporating risk management techniques.

5. The Influence of Inflation:

Inflation erodes purchasing power over time. We discuss the art of accounting for inflation in long-term planning and selecting investments that outpace inflation.

6. The Art of Asset Allocation:

Asset allocation determines portfolio diversification. We explore the art of strategic asset allocation, taking into account risk tolerance, time horizons, and market conditions.

7. The Role of Modern Portfolio Theory (MPT):

MPT guides optimal portfolio construction. We discuss the art of using MPT principles to balance risk and reward through diversified portfolios.

8. The Art of Evaluating Investment Vehicles:

Investment vehicles vary in risk and returns. We explore the art of choosing appropriate investments, including stocks, bonds, mutual funds, ETFs, and alternative assets.

9. The Power of Dollar-Cost Averaging:

Dollar-cost averaging mitigates market timing risks. We discuss the art of systematic investment, making regular contributions to investments over time.

10. The Art of Tax Planning:

Tax planning optimizes after-tax returns. We explore the art of using tax-efficient investments, retirement accounts, and tax-loss harvesting strategies.

11. The Influence of Estate Planning:

Estate planning ensures the smooth transfer of wealth. We discuss the art of creating wills, trusts, and other estate planning tools to protect assets for future generations.

12. The Art of Behavioral Finance in Planning:

Behavioral biases can impact long-term planning. We explore the art of recognizing and mitigating behavioral biases in investment decision-making.

13. The Role of Contingency Planning:

Contingency planning prepares for unexpected events. We discuss the art of creating emergency funds and insurance coverage to safeguard against financial shocks.

14. The Art of Rebalancing:

Rebalancing maintains target asset allocations. We explore the art of periodically adjusting portfolios to realign with original investment objectives.

15. The Power of Regular Review:

Regular review ensures plan efficacy. We discuss the art of conducting periodic portfolio reviews and making adjustments as needed.

16. The Art of Optimizing Fees and Costs:

Minimizing fees enhances investment returns. We explore the art of selecting low-cost investment options and avoiding excessive transaction costs.

17. The Influence of Changing Life Circumstances:

Life changes impact long-term planning. We discuss the art of adapting the plan to evolving life events, such as marriage, childbirth, or career shifts.

18. The Art of Family Financial Education:

Financial education fosters generational wealth. We explore the art of educating family members on long-term planning and investment principles.

19. The Role of Professional Advice:

Professional advice provides expertise and guidance. We discuss the art of seeking financial advisors and wealth managers to optimize long-term planning.

20. The Art of Monitoring Progress:

Monitoring progress ensures plan adherence. We explore the art of tracking financial goals and assessing the plan's effectiveness over time.

Conclusion:

"Building a Masterpiece: Creating a Long-Term Plan" celebrates the art and science of designing a strategic and enduring investment strategy. Just as a master artist carefully plans each element of a masterpiece, successful investors meticulously craft a long-term plan that aligns with their financial goals, risk tolerance, and time horizons. By embracing the art and science of long-term planning, investors can paint a canvas of financial success, combining the creativity of goal setting with the analytical rigor of asset allocation and risk assessment.

In the tapestry of investment success, a well-designed long-term plan becomes the cornerstone, reflecting the fusion of vision, discipline, and adaptability that endures the test of time. By embracing the art and science of long-term planning, investors can paint a canvas of financial success, combining the creativity of goal setting with the analytical rigor of asset allocation and risk assessment. "Building a Masterpiece: Creating a Long-Term Plan" becomes the brushstroke that adds depth, resilience, and purpose to an investment journey, creating a legacy of empowered investors who navigate the complexities of the financial landscape with confidence and foresight.

As the investment landscape continues to evolve, the art of long-term planning will remain essential for navigating changing market conditions and achieving financial security. By carefully curating a long-term plan that encompasses individual financial goals, risk management, and diversified asset allocation, investors can create their financial masterpieces, reflecting their unique aspirations, values, and aspirations. In the tapestry of investment success, "Building a Masterpiece: Creating a Long-Term Plan" becomes the masterpiece, reflecting the fusion of vision, strategy, and adaptability that endures the test of time. The long-term plan becomes a testament to the investor's vision, determination, and commitment to financial prosperity, creating a lasting legacy that reverberates through generations.

CHAPTER 25: THE ART OF TIMING: SEIZING OPPORTUNITIES WISELY

Introduction:

In Chapter 25, "The Art of Timing: Seizing Opportunities Wisely," we delve into the intricacies of making informed decisions in the dynamic world of investing. Just as a skilled artist knows precisely when to add a stroke to the canvas, successful investors possess the ability to identify and capitalize on opportune moments in the market. This chapter explores the art and science of market timing, discussing various approaches, risk considerations, and the importance of discipline and patience in the pursuit of seizing opportunities wisely.

1. Understanding Market Timing:

Market timing refers to the practice of buying and selling assets based on predictions of short-term market movements. We discuss the essence of market timing, its challenges, and its potential benefits.

2. The Art of Fundamental Analysis:

Fundamental analysis involves evaluating the intrinsic value of assets. We explore the art of using financial statements, company performance, and economic indicators to identify undervalued or overvalued investments.

3. The Power of Technical Analysis:

Technical analysis examines historical price and volume patterns to forecast future market movements. We discuss the art of using charts, trendlines, and technical indicators to time entry and exit points.

4. The Influence of Sentiment Analysis:

Sentiment analysis gauges market sentiment and investor emotions. We explore the art of using sentiment indicators to assess market psychology and potential shifts in sentiment.

5. The Art of Contrarian Investing:

Contrarian investors go against prevailing market trends. We discuss the art of contrarian thinking and the potential rewards of buying when others are fearful and selling when others are greedy.

6. The Role of Economic Indicators:

Economic indicators reflect the health of the economy. We explore the art of interpreting economic data and its impact on investment decisions.

7. The Art of Sector Rotation:

Sector rotation involves shifting investments between different sectors. We discuss the art of identifying sectors poised for growth and reallocating assets accordingly.

8. The Power of Seasonal Patterns:

Seasonal patterns influence market behavior. We explore the art of recognizing seasonal trends and using them to guide investment decisions.

9. The Art of Risk Management in Timing:

Market timing involves inherent risks. We discuss the art of managing risk, setting stop-loss orders, and maintaining a diversified portfolio to protect against market downturns.

10. The Influence of Market Liquidity:

Market liquidity affects trade execution and asset prices. We explore the art of navigating illiquid markets and understanding the impact of liquidity on timing decisions.

11. The Art of Trading vs. Investing:

Timing decisions differ for traders and long-term investors. We discuss the art of distinguishing between short-term trading and long-term investing strategies.

12. The Role of Market Sentiment Indicators:

Market sentiment indicators gauge investor optimism and pessimism. We explore the art of using sentiment indicators to validate timing decisions.

13. The Art of Asset Allocation in Timing:

Asset allocation plays a crucial role in timing strategies. We discuss the art of adjusting asset allocation based on market conditions and investment objectives.

14. The Power of Patience in Timing:

Patience is a virtue in timing decisions. We explore the art of waiting for the right opportunities and avoiding impulsive actions.

15. The Art of Dollar-Cost Averaging vs. Lump-Sum Investing:

Dollar-cost averaging and lump-sum investing present different timing approaches. We discuss the art of choosing the appropriate method based on individual circumstances.

16. The Influence of Global Events:

Global events impact market dynamics. We explore the art of factoring geopolitical and macroeconomic events into timing decisions.

17. The Art of Market Timing in Retirement Planning:

Market timing is relevant in retirement planning. We discuss the art of adjusting asset allocation and withdrawal strategies based on market conditions.

18. The Role of Behavioral Finance in Timing:

Behavioral biases influence timing decisions. We explore the art of recognizing and mitigating biases to make rational timing choices.

19. The Art of Staying Informed:

Timely information is critical for market timing. We discuss the art of staying informed through reliable sources and avoiding information overload.

20. The Power of Long-Term Trends:

Long-term trends provide context for timing decisions. We explore the art of identifying enduring trends amidst short-term market noise.

21. The Art of Hedging:

Hedging involves mitigating risk through offsetting positions. We discuss the art of using options and other hedging strategies for timing decisions.

22. The Influence of Central Bank Policies:

Central bank actions impact markets. We explore the art of understanding monetary policy and its effect on timing strategies.

23. The Art of Evaluating Market Valuations:

Market valuations inform timing decisions. We discuss the art of assessing valuations using price-to-earnings ratios and other metrics.

24. The Role of Market Timing in Portfolio Rebalancing:

Market timing can influence portfolio rebalancing. We explore the art of rebalancing during different market conditions.

25. The Art of Exiting Investments:

Knowing when to exit investments is critical. We discuss the art of recognizing signs of a changing market environment and executing timely exits.

Conclusion:

"The Art of Timing: Seizing Opportunities Wisely" celebrates the art and science of making informed decisions in the dynamic world of investing. Just as a skilled artist knows precisely when to add a stroke to the canvas, successful investors possess the ability to identify and capitalize on opportune moments in the market.

In the tapestry of investment success, the art of timing becomes the brushstroke that adds depth, wisdom, and profitability to an investment journey, creating a legacy of empowered investors who navigate market fluctuations with confidence and grace. By embracing the art and science of seizing opportunities wisely, investors can overcome the challenges of market timing, seize advantageous moments, and consistently achieve financial prosperity.

As the investment landscape continues to evolve, the art of timing will remain an essential skill for investors seeking to optimize their returns. By carefully curating timing strategies that encompass fundamental and technical analysis, risk management, and a long-term perspective, investors can create their financial masterpieces, reflecting their unique aspirations, values, and aspirations.

In the tapestry of investment success, "The Art of Timing: Seizing Opportunities Wisely" becomes the masterpiece, reflecting the fusion of vision, discipline, and adaptability that endures the test of time. Just as a master artist carefully plans each element of a masterpiece, successful investors meticulously craft timing strategies that align with their financial goals, risk tolerance, and market outlook.

By embracing the art and science of market timing, investors can paint a canvas of financial success, combining the creativity of timing decisions with the analytical rigor of risk management and portfolio optimization. "The Art of Timing: Seizing Opportunities Wisely" becomes the brushstroke that adds depth, resilience, and purpose to an investment journey, creating a legacy of empowered investors who navigate the complexities of the financial landscape with confidence and foresight. In the tapestry of investment success, "The Art of Timing: Seizing Opportunities Wisely" becomes the masterpiece, reflecting the fusion of vision, strategy, and adaptability that endures the test of time. The art of timing becomes a testament to the investor's vision, determination, and commitment to financial prosperity, creating a lasting legacy that reverberates through generations.

CHAPTER 26: COLORS OF INNOVATION: INVESTING IN EMERGING INDUSTRIES

Introduction:

In Chapter 26, "Colors of Innovation: Investing in Emerging Industries," we immerse ourselves in the world of cutting-edge technologies and industries that hold the potential to reshape the global landscape. Just as colors blend and give life to a vibrant painting, emerging industries add new dimensions to the investment landscape, offering investors opportunities for growth and innovation. This chapter explores the art and science of investing in emerging industries, discussing various sectors, risk considerations, research methodologies, and the importance of a forward-looking perspective in navigating these nascent markets.

1. Understanding Emerging Industries:

Emerging industries encompass the sectors that are in their early stages of development and show significant growth potential. We discuss the essence of emerging industries, their drivers, and the allure they present to forward-thinking investors.

2. The Art of Identifying Promising Sectors:

Identifying promising sectors is akin to selecting colors on a palette. We explore the art of conducting research, analyzing market trends, and recognizing industries poised for disruptive growth.

3. The Power of Technological Advancements:

Technological advancements are the foundation of many

emerging industries. We discuss the art of understanding the impact of technologies such as artificial intelligence, blockchain, and biotechnology on various sectors.

4. The Influence of Regulatory Landscape:

Regulatory factors can shape the trajectory of emerging industries. We explore the art of evaluating regulatory environments and their implications for investments.

5. The Art of Risk Management in Emerging Industries:

Investing in emerging industries carries inherent risks. We discuss the art of managing risks, including market, technology, and regulatory risks, to protect capital.

6. The Role of Venture Capital and Private Equity:

Venture capital and private equity play a vital role in nurturing emerging industries. We explore the art of investing in start-ups and early-stage companies with disruptive potential.

7. The Art of Diversification in Emerging Industries:

Diversification is essential when investing in nascent markets. We discuss the art of building diversified portfolios in emerging industries to mitigate risk.

8. The Power of Innovation and Intellectual Property:

Innovation and intellectual property rights are critical in emerging industries. We explore the art of evaluating companies' intellectual assets and assessing their long-term value.

9. The Art of Investing in Clean Energy:

Clean energy presents a colorful palette of opportunities. We discuss the art of investing in renewable energy, energy storage, and sustainable technologies.

10. The Influence of Biotechnology and Healthcare:

Biotechnology and healthcare are vibrant hues in the world of innovation. We explore the art of investing in biotech companies and breakthrough medical treatments.

11. The Art of Investing in E-commerce and Retail Innovation:

E-commerce and retail innovation are transforming consumer experiences. We discuss the art of investing in companies driving the future of retail and digital commerce.

12. The Role of Space Exploration and Aerospace:

Space exploration and aerospace industries are pushing boundaries. We explore the art of investing in space companies and the future of extraterrestrial endeavors.

13. The Art of Investing in 5G and Connectivity:

Connectivity and 5G technologies open new horizons for innovation. We discuss the art of investing in companies at the forefront of the digital revolution.

14. The Power of Fintech and Digital Finance:

Fintech and digital finance are revolutionizing the financial industry. We explore the art of investing in companies disrupting traditional banking and payment systems.

15. The Art of Investing in Electric and Autonomous Vehicles:

Electric and autonomous vehicles represent a vibrant canvas of transportation. We discuss the art of investing in companies driving the future of mobility.

16. The Influence of Genomics and Precision Medicine:

Genomics and precision medicine are transforming healthcare. We explore the art of investing in companies advancing personalized therapies and genetic research.

17. The Art of Investing in Cybersecurity:

Cybersecurity is an essential layer of protection in the digital era. We discuss the art of investing in companies safeguarding data and information.

18. The Role of Agtech and Food Innovation:

Agtech and food innovation address global challenges in agriculture. We explore the art of investing in companies enhancing food production and sustainability.

19. The Art of Investing in Virtual Reality and Augmented Reality:

Virtual reality and augmented reality offer immersive experiences. We discuss the art of investing in companies shaping the future of entertainment and industrial applications.

20. The Power of Artificial Intelligence and Machine Learning:

Artificial intelligence and machine learning are transforming industries. We explore the art of investing in AI-driven companies and the potential for disruptive applications.

21. The Art of Investing in Robotics and Automation:

Robotics and automation are reshaping industries and workforces. We discuss the art of investing in companies driving efficiency and innovation through automation.

22. The Influence of Environmental, Social, and Governance (ESG) Factors:

ESG considerations are integral to sustainable investing. We explore the art of incorporating ESG principles in emerging industries investments.

23. The Art of Long-Term Perspective in Emerging Industries:

A long-term perspective is vital for investing in emerging industries. We discuss the art of patience and recognizing the gestation period of nascent sectors.

24. The Role of Collaborative Innovation:

Collaborative innovation drives progress in emerging industries. We explore the art of investing in companies that foster partnerships and open innovation, leveraging collective expertise for disruptive advancements.

25. The Art of Investing in Emerging Markets:

Emerging markets offer unique opportunities in emerging industries. We discuss the art of navigating the complexities of investing in developing economies with growth potential.

26. The Power of Industry Disruptors:

Industry disruptors challenge the status quo. We explore the art of identifying disruptor companies and their potential to reshape markets and create new opportunities.

27. The Art of Investing in Impactful Technologies:

Impactful technologies address societal challenges. We discuss the art of investing in companies that prioritize environmental sustainability, social welfare, and positive change.

28. The Influence of Global Mega-Trends:

Global mega-trends shape emerging industries. We explore the art of recognizing and investing in sectors aligned with major demographic, economic, and technological shifts.

29. The Art of Evaluating Management Teams:

Management teams drive success in emerging industries. We discuss the art of assessing leadership quality and their ability to execute on innovative strategies.

30. The Role of Early Adopters and Innovators:

Early adopters and innovators drive market acceptance. We explore the art of identifying companies at the forefront of emerging technologies and trends.

31. The Art of Identifying Market Entry Points:

Timing market entry points is essential in emerging industries. We discuss the art of assessing entry opportunities and taking advantage of favorable risk-reward ratios.

32. The Power of Growth Investing:

Growth investing aligns with emerging industries' potential for rapid expansion. We explore the art of investing in companies with high growth prospects.

33. The Art of Evaluating Market Size and Potential:

Market size determines the scale of opportunities. We discuss the art of assessing market potential and the growth runway for companies in emerging sectors.

34. The Influence of Corporate Innovation Labs:

Corporate innovation labs foster new ideas and technologies. We explore the art of investing in companies with active innovation programs.

35. The Art of Navigating Uncertainty:

Emerging industries entail uncertainty. We discuss the art of managing uncertainty through diversification and disciplined investment practices.

36. The Role of Government Support and Policies:

Government support can boost emerging industries. We explore the art of understanding policy incentives and funding opportunities for innovative companies.

37. The Art of Identifying Competitive Advantages:

Competitive advantages set companies apart in emerging sectors. We discuss the art of identifying firms with sustainable moats and barriers to entry.

38. The Power of Patents and Intellectual Property:

Patents and intellectual property rights safeguard innovations. We explore the art of evaluating the value and protection of intellectual assets.

39. The Art of Sector Forecasting:

Sector forecasting guides investment decisions. We discuss the art of using research and data to project growth trajectories in emerging industries.

40. The Influence of Global Collaboration:

Global collaboration drives innovation in emerging industries. We explore the art of investing in companies with international partnerships and exposure.

41. The Art of Nurturing Innovation Ecosystems:

Innovation ecosystems foster industry growth. We discuss the art of supporting companies that contribute to vibrant innovation communities.

42. The Role of Corporate Venture Capital:

Corporate venture capital fosters industry development. We explore the art of investing in companies backed by established corporations.

43. The Art of Balancing Risk and Reward:

Balancing risk and reward are essential in emerging industries. We discuss the art of managing risk exposure while seeking high-potential opportunities.

44. The Power of Technological Convergence:

Technological convergence drives innovation across sectors. We explore the art of investing in companies at the intersections of multiple emerging technologies.

45. The Art of Identifying Scalability:

Scalability determines companies' growth potential. We discuss the art of assessing scalability in business models of emerging industry companies.

46. The Influence of Education and Research:

Education and research support industry advancements. We explore the art of investing in companies with ties to academic institutions and research centers.

47. The Art of Monitoring Industry Disruptions:

Monitoring industry disruptions informs investment strategies. We discuss the art of staying informed about trends and developments that could impact emerging sectors.

48. The Role of Innovation Incubators:

Innovation incubators nurture start-ups and ideas. We explore the art of investing in companies associated with successful incubator programs.

49. The Art of Embracing Failure:

Failure is a part of innovation. We discuss the art of recognizing that not all investments in emerging industries will succeed and learning from setbacks.

Conclusion:

"Colors of Innovation: Investing in Emerging Industries" celebrates the art and science of investing in nascent sectors that hold the promise of transformational growth. Just as colors blend harmoniously to create a masterpiece, emerging industries add vibrant hues to the investment landscape, offering opportunities for investors to participate in groundbreaking innovations and technologies.

In the tapestry of investment success, the art of investing in emerging industries becomes the brushstroke that adds depth, excitement, and potential to an investment journey, creating a legacy of empowered investors who embrace change and seize opportunities for growth. By embracing the art and science of investing in emerging industries, investors can paint a canvas of financial success, combining the foresight of identifying promising sectors with the analytical rigor of risk management and portfolio diversification.

As the investment landscape continues to evolve, the art of investing in emerging industries will remain a dynamic and rewarding endeavor for those willing to explore uncharted territories and embrace innovation. By carefully curating an investment strategy that encompasses in-depth research, a long-term perspective, and a forward-looking vision, investors can create their financial masterpieces, reflecting their unique aspirations, values, and aspirations.

In the tapestry of investment success, "Colors of Innovation: Investing in Emerging Industries" becomes the masterpiece, reflecting the fusion of vision, discipline, and adaptability that endures the test of time. Just as a master artist carefully plans each element of a masterpiece, successful investors meticulously craft investment strategies that align with the potential of emerging industries, positioning themselves at the forefront of groundbreaking opportunities.

In this chapter, we have explored the art and science of investing in emerging industries, from identifying promising sectors to managing risks and embracing innovation. The world of emerging industries presents a vast spectrum of colors, each representing a unique opportunity for growth and prosperity. As investors navigate this ever-changing landscape, they must combine creativity and vision with rigorous research and analysis to create their financial masterpieces.

Investing in emerging industries requires an adventurous spirit, a willingness to take calculated risks, and an ability to adapt to the dynamic nature of innovation. While the path may be uncertain, the rewards can be immense for those who can identify the trends and companies that will shape the future.

Ultimately, investing in emerging industries is about contributing to the advancement of society, supporting innovative solutions to global challenges, and participating in the growth stories of tomorrow. As technology and human ingenuity continue to push boundaries, the colors of innovation will continue to add richness and diversity to the investment landscape, inspiring a new generation of investors to paint their financial masterpieces with boldness, creativity, and foresight.

CHAPTER 27: UNCONVENTIONAL BRUSHSTROKES: ALTERNATIVE INVESTMENT STRATEGIES

Introduction:

In Chapter 27, "Unconventional Brushstrokes: Alternative Investment Strategies," we delve into the world of alternative investments, which offer unique and unconventional approaches to diversifying portfolios and achieving financial goals. Just as an artist uses unconventional brushstrokes to add texture and depth to their artwork, alternative investments provide investors with non-traditional options that can enhance returns, reduce risk, and bring a new perspective to their investment journey. This chapter explores the art and science of alternative investments, discussing various strategies, risk considerations, benefits, and the importance of integrating these unconventional elements into a well-rounded portfolio.

1. Understanding Alternative Investments:

Alternative investments encompass a wide range of asset classes beyond traditional stocks, bonds, and cash. We discuss the essence of alternative investments, including private equity, hedge funds, real estate, commodities, and more.

2. The Art of Portfolio Diversification:

Diversification is the foundation of alternative investment strategies. We explore the art of using alternative assets to complement traditional holdings and reduce overall portfolio risk.

3. The Power of Non-Correlation:

Alternative investments often exhibit low correlation with traditional assets. We discuss the art of selecting alternative assets that can act as a hedge against market volatility.

4. The Influence of Illiquidity:

Many alternative investments are less liquid than publicly traded assets. We explore the art of managing illiquidity risk and the potential benefits of long-term lockups.

5. The Art of Private Equity Investments:

Private equity offers opportunities to invest in privately-held companies. We discuss the art of evaluating private equity funds and the potential for outsized returns.

6. The Role of Venture Capital:

Venture capital focuses on early-stage companies with high growth potential. We explore the art of investing in start-ups and disruptive technologies.

7. The Art of Hedge Fund Strategies:

Hedge funds employ various strategies, such as long-short, market-neutral, and event-driven. We discuss the art of selecting hedge funds aligned with an investor's risk profile and objectives.

8. The Power of Real Estate:

Real estate provides tangible assets and income-generating potential. We explore the art of investing in commercial properties, residential units, and real estate investment trusts (REITs).

9. The Influence of Commodities:

Commodities add a unique dimension to portfolios. We discuss the art of investing in commodities like gold, oil, and agricultural products to hedge against inflation and geopolitical risks.

10. The Art of Infrastructure Investments:

Infrastructure investments involve projects like toll roads, airports, and energy facilities. We explore the art of investing in essential infrastructure assets with stable cash flows.

11. The Role of Farmland and Timber:

Farmland and timber investments provide exposure to natural resources. We discuss the art of investing in these assets for potential appreciation and diversification.

12. The Art of Collectibles and Rare Assets:

Collectibles, such as art, wine, and rare coins, offer unconventional investment opportunities. We explore the art of investing in tangible assets with cultural and historical significance.

13. The Power of Private Debt:

Private debt involves lending to companies and projects. We discuss the art of investing in private debt for income generation and potential capital appreciation.

14. The Influence of Catastrophe Bonds:

Catastrophe bonds provide insurance coverage against natural disasters. We explore the art of investing in these bonds and their role in risk management.

15. The Art of Cryptocurrency and Digital Assets:

Cryptocurrencies and digital assets present innovative investment opportunities. We discuss the art of understanding this rapidly evolving space and its risks and rewards.

16. The Role of Artificial Intelligence in Alternative Investments:

Artificial intelligence (AI) is transforming alternative investment strategies. We explore the art of using AI-driven algorithms for data analysis and investment decision-making.

17. The Art of Socially Responsible Investing in Alternatives:

Socially responsible investing aligns with alternative strategies. We discuss the art of investing in alternative assets with an ethical and sustainable focus.

18. The Power of Multi-Strategy Funds:

Multi-strategy funds combine various alternative investment approaches. We explore the art of selecting multi-strategy funds for diversified exposure.

19. The Influence of Geographical Diversification:

Alternative investments span global markets. We discuss the art of navigating geopolitical and currency risks through geographical diversification.

20. The Art of Due Diligence in Alternatives:

Due diligence is critical in alternative investments. We explore the art of conducting thorough research and analysis when evaluating alternative assets.

21. The Role of Risk-Adjusted Returns:

Risk-adjusted returns are essential in alternative investments. We discuss the art of assessing risk-adjusted performance to make informed decisions.

22. The Art of Manager Selection:

Selecting skilled managers is vital for alternative strategies. We explore the art of evaluating fund managers' track records, expertise, and alignment with investors' goals.

23. The Power of Private Placements:

Private placements offer access to exclusive investments. We discuss the art of participating in private offerings and their potential benefits.

24. The Influence of Market Cycles:

Market cycles influence alternative investment performance. We explore the art of timing investments to capitalize on market trends.

25. The Art of Tax Efficiency in Alternatives:

Tax efficiency is a consideration in alternative investments. We discuss the art of managing tax implications in alternative assets.

26. The Role of Risk Management in Alternatives:

Risk management is paramount in alternative investment strategies. We explore the art of protecting capital and managing downside risks.

27. The Art of Implementing Alternatives in Portfolios:

Integrating alternatives into portfolios requires strategic planning. We discuss the art of asset allocation and rebalancing with alternative investments.

28. The Power of Customization:

Alternative investments offer customization options. We explore the art of tailoring alternative strategies to meet individual investor preferences.

29. The Influence of Market Sentiment on Alternatives:

Market sentiment impacts alternative asset performance. We discuss the art of recognizing sentiment-driven opportunities and risks.

30. The Art of Exit Strategies:

Exit strategies are essential in alternative investments. We explore the art of realizing profits and exiting positions in illiquid assets.

31. The Role of Family Offices and High-Net-Worth Investors:

Family offices and high-net-worth investors are active in alternatives. We discuss the art of utilizing alternative strategies for wealth preservation and growth.

32. The Art of Integrating Alternatives in Retirement Planning:

Alternatives play a role in retirement planning. We discuss the art of incorporating alternative assets to achieve long-term financial security.

33. The Influence of Regulatory Considerations:

Regulatory factors impact alternative investments. We explore the art of navigating regulatory constraints and compliance requirements.

34. The Art of Investing in Exchange-Traded Funds (ETFs):

ETFs offer alternative exposure to various asset classes. We discuss the art of using ETFs to access alternative investments efficiently.

35. The Power of Market Dislocations:

Market dislocations create alternative investment opportunities. We explore the art of capitalizing on mispricing and market inefficiencies.

36. The Role of Managed Futures:

Managed futures provide exposure to diverse markets. We discuss the art of investing in futures contracts and trend-following strategies.

37. The Art of Evaluating Risk-Reward Profiles:

Risk-reward profiles differ among alternative assets. We explore the art of assessing risk and return characteristics in alternative investment strategies.

38. The Influence of Economic Conditions on Alternatives:

Economic conditions impact alternative assets differently. We discuss the art of tailoring alternative strategies to economic cycles.

39. The Art of Factor Investing in Alternatives:

Factor investing applies to alternative strategies. We explore the art of using factors like value, momentum, and low volatility in alternative portfolios.

40. The Power of Real Assets:

Real assets include tangible properties like infrastructure and natural resources. We discuss the art of investing in real assets for inflation protection and growth potential.

41. The Role of Opportunistic Investments:

Opportunistic investments seek unique opportunities. We explore the art of pursuing specialized deals and strategies.

42. The Art of Investing in Distressed Assets:

Distressed assets present alternative investment opportunities. We discuss the art of investing in distressed debt and assets for potential turnarounds.

43. The Influence of Economic Downturns:

Economic downturns affect alternative investments. We explore the art of managing alternative strategies during economic contractions.

44. The Art of Investing in Farmland and Agriculture:

Farmland and agriculture offer stable returns and diversification. We discuss the art of investing in these essential assets.

45. The Power of Cryptocurrency Funds:

Cryptocurrency funds provide exposure to digital assets. We explore the art of investing in cryptocurrency-focused funds.

46. The Role of Risk Parity Strategies:

Risk parity strategies balance risk across asset classes. We discuss the art of using risk parity in alternative portfolios.

47. The Art of Evaluating Private Real Estate Funds:

Private real estate funds offer access to exclusive properties. We explore the art of assessing real estate fund managers and investment opportunities.

48. The Influence of Institutional Investors:

Institutional investors impact alternative markets. We discuss the art of learning from institutional strategies and positioning accordingly.

49. The Art of Investing in Timberland:

Timberland investments provide long-term growth potential. We explore the art of participating in sustainable timber assets.

50. The Power of Active Management:

Active management is essential in alternative investments. We discuss the art of actively monitoring and adjusting alternative strategies.

Conclusion:

"Unconventional Brushstrokes: Alternative Investment Strategies" celebrates the art and science of diversifying portfolios with unique and unconventional approaches to investing. Just as an artist uses unconventional brushstrokes to add texture and depth to their artwork, alternative investments provide investors with a rich palette of options to enhance returns, reduce risk, and bring a new perspective to their investment journey.

In the tapestry of investment success, the art of alternative investment strategies becomes the brushstroke that adds diversity, creativity, and resilience to an investment journey, creating a legacy of empowered investors who explore unconventional avenues to achieve their financial goals. By embracing the art and science of alternative investments, investors can paint a canvas of financial success, combining traditional wisdom with innovative strategies to create well-rounded and robust portfolios.

As the investment landscape continues to evolve, the art of alternative investments will remain an exciting and dynamic aspect of modern finance. By carefully curating an investment strategy that encompasses alternative assets suited to an investor's risk appetite, return objectives, and time horizon, investors can create their financial masterpieces, reflecting their unique aspirations, values, and aspirations.

In the tapestry of investment success, "Unconventional Brushstrokes: Alternative Investment Strategies" becomes the masterpiece, reflecting the fusion of vision, discipline, and adaptability that endures the test of time. Just as a master artist carefully plans each element of a masterpiece, successful investors meticulously craft alternative investment strategies that align with their financial goals, risk tolerance, and market outlook.

In this chapter, we have explored the art and science of alternative investments, from understanding the diverse range of asset classes to navigating the intricacies of risk and return in unconventional markets. The world of alternative investments offers a vast array of colors, each representing a unique opportunity for investors to explore, innovate, and create diversified portfolios that can weather the uncertainties of the financial landscape.

Investing in alternative strategies requires an open mind, a willingness to explore new frontiers, and a commitment to ongoing research and due diligence. While these brushstrokes may be unconventional, they add depth, richness, and resilience to the investment canvas, empowering investors to create portfolios that reflect their individual vision and investment philosophy.

As the global economy and financial markets continue to evolve, the colors of alternative investments will continue to brighten the investment landscape, inspiring investors to experiment with unconventional strategies and embrace the art of diversification. By embracing alternative investments, investors can add a new layer of creativity and possibility to their portfolios, painting a financial masterpiece that reflects their resilience, vision, and ability to adapt to changing market conditions.

CHAPTER 28: THE ART OF PORTFOLIO REBALANCING

Introduction:

In Chapter 28, "The Art of Portfolio Rebalancing," we embark on a journey to explore the importance and intricacies of maintaining a well-balanced investment portfolio. Much like an artist adjusts the composition of their masterpiece to achieve harmony and coherence, portfolio rebalancing involves realigning asset allocations to ensure that the portfolio remains consistent with an investor's risk tolerance, financial goals, and market conditions. This chapter delves into the art and science of portfolio rebalancing, discussing its benefits, methodologies, best practices, and the role it plays in achieving long-term financial success.

1. Understanding Portfolio Rebalancing:

Portfolio rebalancing is a systematic process of readjusting the allocation of assets in a portfolio to maintain its desired risk and return characteristics. We discuss the essence of portfolio rebalancing and its significance in achieving financial objectives.

2. The Art of Creating a Target Asset Allocation:

Establishing a target asset allocation is the first step in portfolio rebalancing. We explore the art of designing a well-structured portfolio that aligns with an investor's risk tolerance and financial goals.

3. The Power of Diversification:

Diversification is the cornerstone of portfolio rebalancing. We discuss the art of spreading investments across different asset classes to mitigate risk and enhance returns.

4. The Influence of Market Fluctuations:

Market fluctuations can cause deviations from the target asset allocation. We explore the art of identifying triggers for rebalancing based on market movements.

5. The Art of Determining Rebalancing Bands:

Rebalancing bands define the threshold for portfolio adjustments. We discuss the art of setting appropriate bands to trigger rebalancing without excessive turnover.

6. The Role of Risk Tolerance and Investment Horizon:

Risk tolerance and investment horizon impact rebalancing decisions. We explore the art of aligning portfolio adjustments with an investor's risk profile and time horizon.

7. The Art of Tax Efficiency in Rebalancing:

Rebalancing can have tax implications. We discuss the art of executing rebalancing strategies with minimal tax consequences.

8. The Power of Dollar-Cost Averaging:

Dollar-cost averaging can facilitate rebalancing with regular contributions. We explore the art of using this technique to maintain target asset allocations.

9. The Influence of Investor Behavior:

Investor behavior can influence rebalancing decisions. We discuss the art of avoiding emotional biases and adhering to a disciplined rebalancing approach.

10. The Art of Tactical vs. Strategic Rebalancing:

Tactical and strategic rebalancing strategies differ in their approach. We explore the art of choosing the most suitable method for an investor's needs.

11. The Role of Rebalancing Frequency:

Rebalancing frequency impacts portfolio performance. We discuss the art of determining the appropriate frequency based on an investor's objectives.

12. The Art of Asset Allocation Adjustments:

Rebalancing may involve asset allocation adjustments. We explore the art of reallocating assets to capitalize on changing market dynamics.

13. The Power of Risk Management through Rebalancing:

Rebalancing is a risk management tool. We discuss the art of using rebalancing to control portfolio risk and limit exposure to specific asset classes.

14. The Influence of Economic Outlook:

Economic outlook can influence rebalancing decisions. We explore the art of factoring economic conditions into the rebalancing process.

15. The Art of Rebalancing in Retirement Planning:

Rebalancing plays a vital role in retirement planning. We discuss the art of adjusting asset allocations as investors transition into retirement.

16. The Role of Automated Rebalancing Tools:

Automated rebalancing tools simplify the process. We explore the art of using technology to execute rebalancing efficiently.

17. The Art of Rebalancing in Tax-Advantaged Accounts:

Rebalancing in tax-advantaged accounts requires strategic planning. We discuss the art of managing asset allocations while minimizing tax implications.

18. The Power of Rebalancing during Market Crises:

Market crises pose unique challenges for rebalancing. We explore the art of making prudent adjustments during periods of heightened volatility.

19. The Influence of Market Correlations:

Market correlations impact rebalancing decisions. We discuss the art of accounting for correlations when adjusting portfolio allocations.

20. The Art of Rebalancing with Alternatives:

Rebalancing extends to alternative investments. We explore the art of integrating alternative assets into a rebalancing strategy.

21. The Role of Rebalancing with Dividends and Income:

Rebalancing affects income-generating investments. We discuss the art of managing dividends and income distributions during portfolio adjustments.

22. The Art of Rebalancing with Mutual Funds and ETFs:

Rebalancing involves considerations with mutual funds and ETFs. We explore the art of maintaining cost-efficiency and liquidity in fund portfolios.

23. The Power of Dynamic Asset Allocation:

Dynamic asset allocation adjusts to market conditions. We discuss the art of using dynamic strategies in rebalancing.

24. The Influence of Market Momentum:

Market momentum affects rebalancing decisions. We explore the art of navigating momentum-driven trends while maintaining long-term objectives.

25. The Art of Rebalancing in Changing Life Circumstances:

Changing life circumstances may require rebalancing adjustments. We discuss the art of adapting portfolios to evolving financial needs.

26. The Role of Rebalancing in Behavioral Finance:

Behavioral finance principles influence rebalancing decisions. We explore the art of recognizing and managing behavioral biases in portfolio adjustments.

27. The Art of Tactical Asset Allocation:

Tactical asset allocation is a dynamic approach to rebalancing. We discuss the art of incorporating tactical strategies into a long-term investment plan.

28. The Power of Rebalancing with Dollar-Weighted Returns:

Dollar-weighted returns reflect the impact of cash flows. We explore the art of accounting for cash inflows and outflows in rebalancing.

29. The Influence of Economic Indicators:

Economic indicators provide insight into market conditions. We discuss the art of using economic data in rebalancing decisions.

30. The Art of Rebalancing with Concentrated Positions:

Rebalancing can address concentrated positions. We explore the art of diversifying concentrated holdings while considering tax implications.

31. The Role of Rebalancing in Asset Preservation:

Rebalancing supports asset preservation goals. We discuss the art of preserving wealth through disciplined portfolio adjustments.

32. The Art of Rebalancing with Socially Responsible Investments:

Socially responsible investments may require specialized rebalancing strategies. We explore the art of aligning rebalancing with ethical values.

33. The Power of Rebalancing in Market Inefficiencies:

Market inefficiencies present rebalancing opportunities. We discuss the art of capitalizing on mispricing and market anomalies.

34. The Influence of Central Bank Policies:

Central bank policies impact rebalancing decisions. We explore the art of navigating monetary interventions in portfolio adjustments.

35. The Art of Rebalancing in Black Swan Events:

Black swan events challenge rebalancing strategies. We discuss the art of managing unexpected crises with resilience.

36. The Role of Rebalancing with Leveraged and Inverse ETFs:

Rebalancing considerations extend to leveraged and inverse ETFs. We explore the art of using these funds judiciously in rebalancing.

37. The Art of Rebalancing with Algorithmic Strategies:

Algorithmic strategies offer systematic rebalancing solutions. We discuss the art of employing algorithms in portfolio adjustments.

38. The Power of Rebalancing with Factor-Based Investing:

Factor-based investing incorporates systematic factors like value, momentum, and size. We explore the art of integrating factor strategies into the rebalancing process to enhance risk-adjusted returns.

39. The Influence of Behavioral Biases in Rebalancing:

Behavioral biases can hinder effective rebalancing. We discuss the art of recognizing and overcoming biases to execute disciplined portfolio adjustments.

40. The Art of Rebalancing with Global Diversification:

Global diversification enhances portfolio resilience. We explore the art of maintaining a balanced allocation across international markets during rebalancing.

41. The Role of Market Regime Analysis in Rebalancing:

Market regime analysis assesses market conditions. We discuss the art of using this analysis to inform rebalancing decisions.

42. The Art of Monitoring and Tracking Rebalancing:

Regular monitoring and tracking are crucial for successful rebalancing. We explore the art of implementing a systematic process for portfolio adjustments.

43. The Power of Rebalancing to Preserve Risk Tolerance:

Rebalancing maintains an appropriate risk level. We discuss the art of preserving risk tolerance and avoiding portfolio drift through adjustments.

44. The Influence of Market Volatility on Rebalancing:

Market volatility affects the frequency of rebalancing. We explore the art of making measured adjustments in response to market fluctuations.

45. The Art of Rebalancing with Dollar-Cost Ravaging:

Dollar-cost ravaging impacts portfolio withdrawals. We discuss the art of mitigating this risk through strategic rebalancing.

46. The Role of Alternative Investments in Rebalancing:

Alternative investments introduce complexity to rebalancing. We explore the art of integrating alternatives while maintaining target allocations.

47. The Art of Tax-Loss Harvesting in Rebalancing:

Tax-loss harvesting can offset gains and reduce tax liabilities. We discuss the art of leveraging this strategy during rebalancing.

48. The Power of Rebalancing to Control Sequence Risk:

Rebalancing aids in managing sequence risk. We explore the art of minimizing the impact of market fluctuations on portfolio withdrawals.

49. The Influence of Interest Rates on Rebalancing:

Interest rates impact asset returns and correlations. We discuss the art of adapting rebalancing strategies to changing rate environments.

50. The Art of Rebalancing as a Long-Term Discipline:

Rebalancing is a long-term discipline for portfolio management. We explore the art of maintaining focus on long-term objectives while executing periodic adjustments.

Conclusion:

"The Art of Portfolio Rebalancing" celebrates the significance of maintaining a well-balanced investment portfolio through disciplined and thoughtful adjustments. Like an artist perfects their masterpiece with careful adjustments, investors must embrace the art and science of portfolio rebalancing to ensure that their financial goals remain on track amidst changing market conditions.

In the tapestry of investment success, the art of portfolio rebalancing becomes the brushstroke that adds precision, resilience, and adaptability to an investment journey, creating a legacy of empowered investors who understand the importance of maintaining a diversified and risk-appropriate portfolio. By embracing the art and science of portfolio rebalancing, investors can create a financial masterpiece that reflects their ability to navigate market fluctuations and achieve long-term financial prosperity.

As the investment landscape continues to evolve, the colors of portfolio rebalancing will remain an evergreen aspect of sound investment strategies. By carefully curating a rebalancing process that aligns with an investor's unique risk profile, financial goals, and market outlook, investors can create their financial masterpieces, reflecting their vision, discipline, and resilience in the face of changing market dynamics.

In this chapter, we have explored the art and science of portfolio rebalancing, from understanding its importance to implementing effective strategies. The world of portfolio management offers a rich palette of colors, each representing a unique opportunity for investors to realign their portfolios and maintain the desired risk and return characteristics.

Portfolio rebalancing requires a methodical approach, a

commitment to disciplined execution, and a focus on long-term objectives. By embracing the art of portfolio rebalancing, investors can add a new layer of precision and control to their portfolios, enabling them to weather market storms and pursue their financial aspirations with confidence.

Just as artists refine their masterpieces through precise brushstrokes, investors refine their portfolios through strategic rebalancing, ensuring that their investments remain aligned with their evolving financial needs and risk appetite. As investors continue their journey toward financial success, the art of portfolio rebalancing will stand as a testament to their ability to adapt, grow, and paint a canvas of financial prosperity that endures the test of time.

CHAPTER 29: NAVIGATING THE STORM: INVESTING IN TURBULENT TIMES

Introduction:

In Chapter 29, "Navigating the Storm: Investing in Turbulent Times," we delve into the art and science of investing during periods of market turmoil and economic uncertainty. Much like a seasoned sailor navigates stormy seas with skill and composure, successful investors must weather financial storms with resilience and strategic decision-making. This chapter explores the challenges and opportunities presented by turbulent times, the various strategies to mitigate risk and capitalize on market dislocations, and the importance of maintaining a long-term perspective amidst short-term volatility.

1. Understanding Turbulent Times:

Turbulent times encompass periods of heightened market volatility, economic downturns, geopolitical tensions, and unexpected events. We discuss the essence of turbulent markets and their impact on investor psychology.

2. The Art of Embracing Uncertainty:

Embracing uncertainty is key to navigating turbulent times. We explore the art of remaining composed and objective during periods of market instability.

3. The Power of Crisis Preparedness:

Crisis preparedness is vital for investors. We discuss the art of building robust portfolios and contingency plans to withstand adverse market conditions.

4. The Influence of Behavioral Biases in Turbulent Markets:

Behavioral biases can drive irrational decision-making during turbulent times. We explore the art of recognizing and overcoming biases to make informed choices.

5. The Art of Portfolio Stress Testing:

Stress testing assesses portfolio resilience under extreme scenarios. We discuss the art of stress testing to identify potential weaknesses and improve risk management.

6. The Role of Asset Allocation in Turbulent Markets:

Asset allocation becomes crucial in turbulent times. We explore the art of strategically diversifying investments to manage risk and capitalize on opportunities.

7. The Art of Defensive Investing:

Defensive investing focuses on stable and low-volatility assets. We discuss the art of building defensive portfolios to protect capital during market downturns.

8. The Power of Quality Investing:

Quality investing emphasizes strong fundamentals and stability. We explore the art of investing in high-quality companies during turbulent times.

9. The Influence of Active vs. Passive Investing in Turbulent Markets:

Active and passive investing approaches differ in turbulent times. We discuss the art of blending both strategies for optimal risk-adjusted returns.

10. The Art of Contrarian Investing:

Contrarian investing seeks opportunities in unloved assets. We explore the art of contrarian thinking during turbulent times to uncover undervalued investments.

11. The Role of Gold and Precious Metals:

Gold and precious metals act as safe-haven assets. We discuss the art of including these assets in portfolios to hedge against market uncertainty.

12. The Art of Investing in Defensive Sectors:

Defensive sectors perform well in turbulent markets. We explore the art of allocating to defensive industries that demonstrate resilience.

13. The Power of Dividend Investing:

Dividend investing provides income stability. We discuss the art of investing in dividend-paying companies during periods of economic uncertainty.

14. The Influence of Central Bank Policies on Turbulent Markets:

Central bank policies impact turbulent markets. We explore the art of understanding monetary interventions and their implications for investments.

15. The Art of Navigating Market Volatility:

Market volatility requires a measured approach. We discuss the art of staying calm and making strategic decisions amid turbulent market swings.

16. The Role of Hedging Strategies:

Hedging strategies protect against downside risk. We explore the art of using hedging instruments like options and futures during turbulent times.

17. The Art of Tactical Asset Allocation:

Tactical asset allocation adapts to market conditions. We discuss the art of making timely adjustments to asset allocations during turbulent times.

18. The Power of Diversification during Market Turmoil:

Diversification reduces portfolio concentration risk. We explore the art of diversifying across asset classes and geographies in turbulent markets.

19. The Influence of Geopolitical Risks:

Geopolitical risks impact global markets. We discuss the art of managing geopolitical uncertainties and their implications for investments.

20. The Art of Contingency Planning:

Contingency planning prepares for unforeseen events. We explore the art of creating contingency plans to address potential risks.

21. The Role of Long-Term Investing in Turbulent Times:

Long-term investing maintains focus during short-term volatility. We discuss the art of staying committed to long-term goals amid market fluctuations.

22. The Art of Recognizing Market Opportunities:

Turbulent times present unique investment opportunities. We explore the art of identifying attractive investments during market dislocations.

23. The Power of Fundamental Analysis in Turbulent Markets:

Fundamental analysis provides insights into company valuations. We discuss the art of using fundamental analysis to make informed investment decisions.

24. The Influence of Technical Analysis on Turbulent Markets:

Technical analysis assesses market trends and price patterns. We explore the art of using technical analysis to identify entry and exit points.

25. The Art of Behavioral Finance in Turbulent Markets:

Behavioral finance principles apply in turbulent times. We discuss the art of managing emotions and biases to make rational investment choices.

26. The Role of Systematic Investment Plans (SIPs):

SIPs provide disciplined investing during turbulent times. We explore the art of using SIPs to accumulate wealth amid market volatility.

27. The Art of Leveraging Market Volatility:

Market volatility creates trading opportunities. We discuss the art of using volatility to enhance returns through strategic trades.

28. The Power of Emerging Market Opportunities:

Emerging markets offer growth potential. We explore the art of diversifying into emerging markets during turbulent times.

29. The Influence of Technological Disruptions:

Technological disruptions impact industries and investments. We discuss the art of investing in innovative companies during periods of disruption.

30. The Art of Anticipating Market Inflection Points:

Market inflection points signal reversals in trends. We explore the art of anticipating and positioning for market turning points.

31. The Role of Active Risk Management:

Active risk management protects portfolios from severe losses. We discuss the art of proactively managing risk during turbulent times.

32. The Art of Behavioral Coaching in Volatile Markets:

Behavioral coaching supports disciplined investing. We explore the art of providing guidance to investors during turbulent times.

33. The Power of Long-Term Value Investing:

Long-term value investing transcends short-term volatility. We discuss the art of seeking undervalued assets with strong long-term potential.

34. The Influence of Black Swan Events on Investments:

Black swan events are rare and impactful. We explore the art of preparing for unexpected shocks in financial markets.

35. The Art of Defensive Asset Allocation:

Defensive asset allocation seeks to protect capital during turbulent times. We discuss the art of allocating to safe-haven assets like bonds and cash.

36. The Role of Market Liquidity in Turbulent Markets:

Market liquidity affects asset prices and trading volumes. We explore the art of navigating illiquid markets during turbulent times.

37. The Art of Managing Margin and Leverage:

Margin and leverage amplify both gains and losses. We discuss the art of prudently managing margin and leverage during market volatility.

38. The Power of Human Capital in Turbulent Times:

Human capital is an essential asset during uncertain times. We explore the art of recognizing the value of skills, knowledge, and adaptability in turbulent markets.

39. The Influence of Inflation and Deflation on Investments:

Inflation and deflation impact asset values differently. We discuss the art of positioning investments to hedge against inflationary and deflationary pressures.

40. The Art of Tactical Sector Rotation:

Sector rotation adapts to changing market dynamics. We explore the art of rotating investments among sectors to capitalize on shifting trends.

41. The Role of Market Sentiment in Turbulent Markets:

Market sentiment can drive irrational behavior. We discuss the art of using contrarian strategies based on market sentiment indicators.

42. The Art of Staying Invested in Turbulent Times:

Staying invested maintains exposure to long-term growth. We explore the art of resisting the temptation to time the market and adhering to a disciplined approach.

43. The Power of Investor Education during Market Uncertainty:

Investor education enhances decision-making during turbulent times. We discuss the art of empowering investors with knowledge and information.

44. The Influence of Government Policies on Investments:

Government policies impact financial markets. We explore the art of adapting investment strategies to align with policy changes.

45. The Art of Ethical Investing in Turbulent Times:

Ethical investing reflects values and principles. We discuss the art of aligning investments with social and environmental objectives during market uncertainty.

46. The Role of Professional Advice in Turbulent Markets:

Professional advice provides guidance during uncertain times. We explore the art of seeking expert counsel to navigate complex market conditions.

47. The Art of Analyzing Company Resilience:

Company resilience reflects stability and adaptability. We discuss the art of assessing a company's ability to weather turbulent economic conditions.

48. The Power of Cash as a Strategic Asset:

Cash offers flexibility and opportunity in volatile markets. We explore the art of strategically holding cash to seize investment opportunities.

49. The Influence of Currency Risk in Turbulent Markets:

Currency risk impacts international investments. We discuss the art of managing currency exposures during market turbulence.

50. The Art of Learning from Past Turbulent Times:

History provides lessons for navigating turbulent markets. We explore the art of drawing insights from past financial crises and economic downturns.

Conclusion:

"Navigating the Storm: Investing in Turbulent Times" celebrates the resilience and adaptability of investors in the face of challenging market conditions. Just as a seasoned sailor steers through rough waters with skill and determination, successful investors navigate turbulent markets with prudence, discipline, and a long-term perspective. By embracing the art and science of investing during turbulent times, investors can weather market storms, capitalize on opportunities, and ultimately achieve their financial goals.

In the tapestry of investment success, the art of navigating turbulent times becomes the brushstroke that adds depth, wisdom, and foresight to an investment journey. As investors navigate through periods of market turmoil and economic uncertainty, they become adept at recognizing when to weather the storm and when to seize opportunities. By embracing the art and science of investing during turbulent times, investors can paint a financial masterpiece that reflects their ability to endure, grow, and achieve financial prosperity despite the ebb and flow of markets.

As the investment landscape continues to evolve, the colors of turbulent markets will remain an integral part of the investor's palette. By carefully curating an investment approach that incorporates strategies to manage risk, capitalize on opportunities, and maintain a long-term outlook, investors can create their financial masterpieces, reflecting their resilience, vision, and ability to navigate through turbulent times with poise.

In this chapter, we have explored the art and science of investing during turbulent times, from understanding the challenges to implementing strategic responses. The world of investing during market uncertainty offers a rich array of colors, each representing an opportunity for investors to showcase their ability to stay composed, adapt, and thrive amidst market fluctuations.

Investing during turbulent times requires courage, patience, and a willingness to learn from past experiences. By embracing the art of navigating the storm, investors can add a new layer of skill and wisdom to their portfolios, enabling them to navigate through market uncertainty with confidence and achieve their long-term financial aspirations. Just as skilled sailors emerge stronger after navigating stormy seas, successful investors emerge wiser and more resilient after navigating turbulent markets, painting a legacy of financial success that withstands the test of time.

CHAPTER 30: THE ART OF PORTFOLIO OPTIMIZATION

Introduction:

In Chapter 30, "The Art of Portfolio Optimization," we embark on a journey to explore the intricate process of creating an efficient investment portfolio that maximizes returns while minimizing risk. Just as a skilled artist carefully selects and blends colors to create a masterpiece, portfolio optimization involves the meticulous selection and allocation of assets to achieve an ideal balance of risk and reward. This chapter delves into the principles of portfolio optimization, the various methodologies used, the role of diversification, and the importance of tailoring portfolios to individual investor objectives.

1. Understanding Portfolio Optimization:

Portfolio optimization is the process of constructing an investment portfolio that aims to achieve the best possible risk-adjusted return. We discuss the essence of portfolio optimization and its significance in achieving financial goals.

2. The Art of Defining Investment Objectives:

Investment objectives differ among investors. We explore the art of defining clear and measurable objectives as the foundation of portfolio optimization.

3. The Power of Modern Portfolio Theory (MPT):

Modern Portfolio Theory revolutionized portfolio optimization. We discuss the art of using MPT to identify the optimal combination of assets for a given level of risk.

4. The Influence of Risk and Return:

Risk and return are fundamental drivers of portfolio optimization. We explore the art of striking a balance between risk appetite and return expectations.

5. The Art of Efficient Frontier Analysis:

Efficient Frontier Analysis identifies optimal portfolios. We discuss the art of plotting efficient frontiers to visualize trade-offs between risk and return.

6. The Role of Correlation and Diversification:

Correlation affects portfolio diversification. We explore the art of diversifying across assets with low correlation to reduce overall portfolio risk.

7. The Art of Asset Allocation:

Asset allocation is the cornerstone of portfolio optimization. We discuss the art of allocating investments among different asset classes to achieve desired risk-return profiles.

8. The Power of Mean-Variance Optimization:

Mean-Variance Optimization maximizes return for a given level of risk. We explore the art of using this mathematical approach to construct efficient portfolios.

9. The Influence of Expected Return Estimation:

Expected return estimation impacts portfolio optimization. We discuss the art of using historical data, financial models, and expert judgment to estimate returns.

10. The Art of Risk Estimation:

Risk estimation is critical for portfolio optimization. We explore the art of using standard deviation, value at risk (VaR), and other metrics to measure risk.

11. The Role of Capital Market Assumptions:

Capital market assumptions shape portfolio optimization. We discuss the art of using realistic assumptions to build robust investment strategies.

12. The Art of Incorporating Investor Constraints:

Investor constraints impact portfolio optimization. We explore the art of considering factors like liquidity needs, time horizon, and tax implications.

13. The Power of Black-Litterman Model:

The Black-Litterman Model improves return forecasts. We discuss the art of using this model to adjust portfolio weights based on market views.

14. The Influence of Monte Carlo Simulation:

Monte Carlo Simulation tests portfolio performance under different scenarios. We explore the art of using simulation to assess robustness and sensitivity.

15. The Art of Optimizing Risk Parity:

Risk Parity aims for equal risk contributions across assets. We discuss the art of implementing this approach to diversify risk effectively.

16. The Role of Bayesian Optimization:

Bayesian Optimization refines portfolio selection. We explore the art of using Bayesian techniques to identify optimal asset allocations.

17. The Art of Handling Non-Normal Distributions:

Non-normal distributions challenge portfolio optimization. We discuss the art of adapting methods for skewed or fat-tailed return distributions.

18. The Power of Robo-Advisors in Portfolio Optimization:

Robo-advisors automate portfolio optimization. We explore the art of leveraging technology to create customized and efficient portfolios.

19. The Influence of Transaction Costs:

Transaction costs impact portfolio optimization. We discuss

the art of minimizing costs to enhance overall portfolio performance.

20. The Art of Portfolio Rebalancing in Optimization:

Portfolio rebalancing maintains optimal allocations. We explore the art of incorporating rebalancing in the optimization process.

21. The Role of Tax Efficiency in Optimization:

Tax efficiency enhances after-tax returns. We discuss the art of optimizing portfolios while considering tax implications.

22. The Art of Factor-Based Portfolio Optimization:

Factor-Based Portfolio Optimization focuses on risk factors. We explore the art of constructing factor-based portfolios to achieve specific objectives.

23. The Power of Multi-Objective Optimization:

Multi-Objective Optimization accommodates multiple goals. We discuss the art of finding trade-offs between conflicting objectives.

24. The Influence of Environmental, Social, and Governance (ESG) Factors:

ESG factors influence portfolio optimization. We explore the art of integrating ESG criteria in portfolio construction.

25. The Art of Tailoring Portfolios to Investor Risk Profile:

Investor risk profile guides portfolio optimization. We discuss the art of matching portfolios to individual risk preferences.

26. The Role of Systematic vs. Discretionary Approaches:

Systematic and discretionary approaches differ in optimization. We explore the art of choosing the most suitable method for portfolio construction.

27. The Art of Optimizing Across Asset Classes:

Optimizing across asset classes is complex. We discuss the art of balancing allocations across diverse assets.

28. The Power of Robust Optimization:

Robust Optimization considers uncertainties in inputs. We explore the art of constructing portfolios that withstand market variations.

29. The Influence of Scenario-Based Optimization:

Scenario-Based Optimization accounts for diverse scenarios. We discuss the art of stress-testing portfolios using scenario analysis.

30. The Art of Applying Artificial Intelligence in Optimization:

Artificial Intelligence enhances portfolio optimization. We explore the art of using machine learning and AI algorithms for data-driven decisions.

31. The Role of Portfolio Constraints in Optimization:

Portfolio constraints shape optimization outcomes. We discuss the art of managing constraints to achieve desired outcomes.

32. The Art of Dynamic Portfolio Optimization:

Dynamic Portfolio Optimization adapts to changing conditions. We explore the art of adjusting portfolios in response to market shifts.

33. The Power of Multi-Asset Class Optimization:

Multi-Asset Class Optimization involves diverse assets. We discuss the art of balancing risks and returns across various asset classes.

34. The Influence of Economic Regime-Based Optimization:

Economic Regime-Based Optimization adjusts to economic cycles. We explore the art of aligning portfolios with different economic environments.

35. The Art of Stress Testing and Sensitivity Analysis:

Stress testing assesses portfolio resilience. We discuss the art of using sensitivity analysis to evaluate risk exposures.

36. The Role of Machine Learning in Portfolio Optimization:

Machine Learning enhances optimization models. We explore the art of using ML algorithms to improve portfolio construction.

37. The Art of Long-Short Portfolio Optimization:

Long-Short Portfolio Optimization involves both long and short positions. We discuss the art of creating market-neutral strategies.

38. The Power of Risk Budgeting in Portfolio Optimization:

Risk Budgeting allocates risk across assets. We explore the art of managing risk allocations for better diversification.

39. The Influence of Investment Constraints in Optimization:

Investment constraints impact optimization strategies. We discuss the art of accommodating constraints while optimizing portfolios.

40. The Art of Combining Active and Passive Strategies:

Combining active and passive strategies diversifies portfolios. We explore the art of blending both approaches for optimal outcomes.

41. The Role of Factor Timing in Portfolio Optimization:

Factor Timing adjusts factor exposures. We discuss the art of incorporating factor timing strategies in optimization.

42. The Art of Utilizing Factor Tilts:

Factor Tilts overweight specific factors. We explore the art of using tilts to enhance risk-adjusted returns and capture potential market premiums.

43. The Power of Scenario Analysis in Optimization:

Scenario Analysis assesses portfolio performance under various scenarios. We discuss the art of using this technique to enhance decision-making.

44. The Influence of Monte Carlo Simulation in Portfolio Optimization:

Monte Carlo Simulation aids in portfolio stress testing. We explore the art of using simulation to model thousands of possible market outcomes.

45. The Art of Bayesian Optimization in Portfolio Construction:

Bayesian Optimization optimizes portfolios based on prior knowledge. We discuss the art of leveraging Bayesian methods to handle uncertainty.

46. The Role of Evolutionary Algorithms in Portfolio Optimization:

Evolutionary Algorithms mimic natural selection to optimize portfolios. We explore the art of using genetic algorithms to find optimal solutions.

47. The Art of Portfolio Insurance:

Portfolio Insurance protects against severe losses. We discuss the art of using dynamic hedging strategies during market downturns.

48. The Power of Risk Parity and Equal Weighting:

Risk Parity and Equal Weighting offer alternative weighting methods. We explore the art of implementing these approaches for diversification.

49. The Influence of Regime-Switching Models in Optimization:

Regime-Switching Models adapt portfolios to changing market conditions. We discuss the art of incorporating these models for dynamic allocations.

50. The Art of Integrating Behavioral Finance in Portfolio Optimization:

Behavioral Finance principles influence investor decision-making. We explore the art of accounting for behavioral biases in portfolio construction.

Conclusion:

"The Art of Portfolio Optimization" celebrates the intricacies of crafting investment portfolios that align with individual goals, risk tolerances, and market conditions. Like a skilled artist who skillfully combines colors and textures to create a masterpiece, successful portfolio managers carefully blend assets and investment strategies to achieve optimal risk-adjusted returns. By embracing the art and science of portfolio optimization, investors can create financial masterpieces that reflect their unique financial aspirations, values, and risk appetites.

In the tapestry of investment success, the art of portfolio optimization becomes the brushstroke that adds precision, balance, and adaptability to an investment journey. As investors navigate through the complexities of financial markets and seek to achieve their financial objectives, the art of portfolio optimization remains a guiding principle that enables them to navigate market fluctuations, mitigate risks, and capitalize on opportunities.

As the investment landscape continues to evolve, the colors of portfolio optimization will remain an integral part of the investor's palette. By carefully curating a portfolio optimization process that aligns with individual investor preferences and market outlook, investors can create their financial masterpieces, reflecting their vision, discipline, and ability to adapt to ever-changing market dynamics.

In this chapter, we have explored the art and science of portfolio optimization, from understanding its principles to applying various methodologies. The world of portfolio management offers a diverse array of colors, each representing a unique approach to achieving financial goals. By embracing the art of portfolio optimization, investors can add a new layer of sophistication and creativity to their portfolios, enabling them to navigate through market uncertainties, achieve their financial aspirations, and create a lasting legacy of financial prosperity.

CHAPTER 31: THE PSYCHOLOGY OF MARKET SENTIMENT

Introduction:

In Chapter 31, "The Psychology of Market Sentiment," we delve into the fascinating world of investor psychology and how it influences market sentiment, driving market behavior and impacting asset prices. Just as a skilled artist understands the intricacies of human emotions and uses them to evoke specific responses, understanding market sentiment is crucial for investors to make informed decisions. This chapter explores the various psychological factors that shape market sentiment, the role of behavioral biases, and the art of managing emotions to achieve better investment outcomes.

1. Understanding Market Sentiment:

Market sentiment refers to the overall attitude and mood of investors towards financial markets and specific assets. We discuss the essence of market sentiment and its impact on market dynamics.

2. The Power of Greed and Fear:

Greed and fear are dominant emotions in financial markets. We explore the art of recognizing these emotions and managing their influence on investment decisions.

3. The Influence of Herding Behavior:

Herding behavior leads to crowd-following in markets. We discuss the art of understanding herding and its implications for asset prices.

4. The Art of Contrarian Investing:

Contrarian investors go against the crowd. We explore the art of embracing contrarian thinking to identify opportunities amid market sentiment extremes.

5. The Role of Overconfidence Bias:

Overconfidence bias leads to unwarranted risk-taking. We discuss the art of avoiding overconfidence and maintaining realistic expectations.

6. The Art of Fear of Missing Out (FOMO):

FOMO drives impulsive decision-making. We explore the art of managing FOMO to avoid speculative and irrational investments.

7. The Power of Confirmation Bias:

Confirmation bias leads to selective information processing. We discuss the art of seeking diverse perspectives to avoid biased judgments.

8. The Influence of Anchoring Bias:

Anchoring bias fixates on irrelevant information. We explore the art of recognizing and overcoming anchoring in investment analysis.

9. The Art of Loss Aversion:

Loss aversion leads to risk aversion in investing. We discuss the art of managing loss aversion to maintain a balanced portfolio.

10. The Role of Availability Bias:

Availability bias relies on readily available information. We explore the art of conducting thorough research to avoid biased decisions.

11. The Art of Regret Aversion:

Regret aversion hinders decision-making. We discuss the art of accepting losses and learning from mistakes to improve investment outcomes.

12. The Power of Hindsight Bias:

Hindsight bias distorts perceptions of past events. We explore the art of recognizing hindsight bias and making objective decisions.

13. The Influence of Mental Accounting:

Mental accounting segregates funds based on origin. We discuss the art of adopting a holistic view of investments for optimal portfolio management.

14. The Art of Framing Effects:

Framing effects impact decision-making based on presentation. We explore the art of analyzing information objectively, regardless of framing.

15. The Role of Prospect Theory:

Prospect theory explains risk preferences. We discuss the art of applying prospect theory to understand investor behavior.

16. The Art of Managing Emotional Biases:

Emotional biases hinder rational decision-making. We explore the art of managing emotions to make objective investment choices.

17. The Power of Self-Control:

Self-control reduces impulsive actions. We discuss the art of exercising self-control to adhere to investment strategies.

18. The Influence of Investor Sentiment Indicators:

Investor sentiment indicators gauge market mood. We explore the art of using sentiment indicators to identify potential market turning points.

19. The Art of Sentiment Analysis in Social Media:

Social media impacts market sentiment. We discuss the art of sentiment analysis to assess public opinions on financial assets.

20. The Role of Media and News in Shaping Sentiment:

Media narratives influence market sentiment. We explore the

art of critically analyzing media coverage to avoid biased perspectives.

21. The Art of Behavioral Finance:

Behavioral finance combines psychology and finance. We discuss the art of applying behavioral finance principles in investment strategies.

22. The Power of Cognitive Biases in Trading:

Cognitive biases influence trading decisions. We explore the art of recognizing and managing cognitive biases to enhance trading outcomes.

23. The Influence of Groupthink:

Groupthink leads to irrational consensus decisions. We discuss the art of avoiding groupthink in investment committees and decision-making.

24. The Art of Emotionally Intelligent Investing:

Emotional intelligence enhances decision-making. We explore the art of developing emotional intelligence for better investment outcomes.

25. The Role of Regret in Investment Decisions:

Regret affects decision-making under uncertainty. We discuss the art of minimizing regret to avoid impulsive actions.

26. The Art of Mindful Investing:

Mindful investing cultivates awareness of emotions. We explore the art of practicing mindfulness to make calm and rational investment decisions.

27. The Power of Patience and Discipline:

Patience and discipline are key to successful investing. We discuss the art of staying disciplined and avoiding knee-jerk reactions.

28. The Influence of Market Noise:

Market noise creates distractions. We explore the art of filtering out noise to focus on relevant market information.

29. The Art of Controlling Emotions during Market Volatility:

Market volatility triggers emotional responses. We discuss the art of staying composed during turbulent market conditions.

30. The Role of Behavioral Finance in Risk Management:

Behavioral finance enhances risk management. We explore the art of using behavioral finance insights to improve risk assessment.

31. The Art of Learning from Past Market Sentiments:

History provides insights into market sentiment. We discuss the art of learning from past market behavior to anticipate future trends.

Conclusion:

"The Psychology of Market Sentiment" celebrates the intricate interplay between human emotions and financial markets. Just as a skilled artist understands the power of colors and brushstrokes to evoke emotions in their art, successful investors comprehend the significance of market sentiment in shaping investment decisions. By embracing the art and science of understanding market sentiment, investors can navigate through the complexities of financial markets with greater awareness, rationality, and resilience.

In the tapestry of investment success, the psychology of market sentiment becomes the brushstroke that adds depth, context, and precision to an investment journey. As investors seek to make prudent decisions amidst the turbulence of financial markets, the psychology of market sentiment remains a guiding principle that enables them to recognize biases, manage emotions, and make informed choices based on sound analysis.

CHAPTER 32: THE ART OF READING FINANCIAL STATEMENTS

Introduction:

In Chapter 32, "The Art of Reading Financial Statements," we embark on a comprehensive exploration of financial statements, the vital documents that provide a window into a company's financial health. Just as a skilled artist meticulously examines the details and nuances of a masterpiece, investors must develop the ability to read and interpret financial statements to make informed investment decisions. This chapter delves into the key components of financial statements, the art of analyzing ratios and trends, and the significance of financial statement analysis in evaluating a company's performance and prospects.

1. Understanding Financial Statements:

Financial statements are the backbone of corporate reporting. We discuss the essence of financial statements and their role in providing a snapshot of a company's financial position and performance.

2. The Balance Sheet - Unraveling a Company's Financial Position:

The balance sheet displays a company's assets, liabilities, and equity. We explore the art of understanding the balance sheet to assess solvency and liquidity.

3. The Income Statement - Unveiling a Company's Performance:

The income statement presents a company's revenue, expenses, and profits. We discuss the art of analyzing the income statement to evaluate profitability.

4. The Cash Flow Statement - Tracking a Company's Cash Flows:

The cash flow statement reveals a company's cash inflows and outflows. We explore the art of interpreting the cash flow statement to assess liquidity and cash management.

5. The Art of Understanding Notes to Financial Statements:

Notes provide critical context to financial statements. We discuss the art of reading and analyzing notes to gain deeper insights into a company's financials.

6. The Role of Auditor's Reports:

Auditor's reports validate financial statements. We explore the art of interpreting auditor's reports to understand the level of assurance provided.

7. The Art of Interpreting Accounting Policies:

Accounting policies impact financial reporting. We discuss the art of understanding accounting policies to ensure consistency in analysis.

8. The Power of Financial Statement Analysis:

Financial statement analysis helps evaluate a company's performance. We explore the art of using analysis to make informed investment decisions.

9. The Influence of Horizontal Analysis:

Horizontal analysis compares financial data over time. We discuss the art of conducting horizontal analysis to identify trends and changes.

10. The Art of Vertical Analysis:

Vertical analysis compares financial data as a percentage of total assets or revenues. We explore the art of using vertical analysis to assess cost structures and profitability.

11. The Role of Ratio Analysis:

Ratio analysis evaluates relationships between financial data. We discuss the art of analyzing ratios to measure liquidity, solvency, efficiency, and profitability.

12. The Art of Liquidity Analysis:

Liquidity ratios assess a company's ability to meet short-term obligations. We explore the art of using liquidity ratios to gauge financial health.

13. The Power of Solvency Analysis:

Solvency ratios evaluate a company's long-term stability. We discuss the art of using solvency ratios to assess a company's ability to meet long-term obligations.

14. The Influence of Efficiency Analysis:

Efficiency ratios measure a company's operational effectiveness. We explore the art of using efficiency ratios to evaluate productivity and resource utilization.

15. The Art of Profitability Analysis:

Profitability ratios assess a company's ability to generate profits. We discuss the art of using profitability ratios to understand financial performance.

16. The Role of DuPont Analysis:

DuPont Analysis dissects return on equity (ROE). We explore the art of using DuPont Analysis to understand drivers of profitability.

17. The Art of Using Price-to-Earnings (P/E) Ratio:

The P/E ratio compares a company's share price to earnings per share. We discuss the art of using P/E ratio to assess valuation.

18. The Power of Price-to-Book (P/B) Ratio:

The P/B ratio compares a company's share price to book value per share. We explore the art of using P/B ratio to evaluate a company's assets' relative worth.

19. The Influence of Price-to-Sales (P/S) Ratio:

The P/S ratio compares a company's share price to revenue per share. We discuss the art of using P/S ratio to assess a company's sales efficiency.

20. The Art of Using Price-to-Cash Flow (P/CF) Ratio:

The P/CF ratio compares a company's share price to cash flow per share. We explore the art of using P/CF ratio to evaluate a company's cash generation.

21. The Role of Dividend Yield:

Dividend yield measures a company's dividend payout relative to its share price. We discuss the art of using dividend yield to assess income generation.

22. The Art of Analyzing Earnings per Share (EPS):

EPS reflects a company's profitability on a per-share basis. We explore the art of using EPS to evaluate earnings performance.

23. The Power of Return on Equity (ROE):

ROE measures a company's profitability in relation to shareholder equity. We discuss the art of using ROE to assess a company's efficiency in generating profits.

24. The Influence of Debt-to-Equity (D/E) Ratio:

The D/E ratio compares a company's debt to its equity. We explore the art of using D/E ratio to evaluate a company's leverage and financial risk.

25. The Art of Assessing Current Ratio:

The current ratio measures a company's ability to meet short-term obligations. We discuss the art of using the current ratio to assess liquidity.

26. The Role of Quick Ratio:

The quick ratio assesses a company's ability to meet short-term obligations without relying on inventory. We explore the art of using the quick ratio to evaluate liquidity.

27. The Art of Analyzing Inventory Turnover:

Inventory turnover measures how quickly a company sells its inventory. We discuss the art of using inventory turnover to assess inventory management.

28. The Power of Days Sales Outstanding (DSO):

DSO measures the average time it takes a company to collect revenue from sales. We explore the art of using DSO to evaluate the efficiency of credit management.

29. The Influence of Days Payable Outstanding (DPO):

DPO measures the average time it takes a company to pay its suppliers. We discuss the art of using DPO to assess cash management.

30. The Art of Analyzing Fixed Asset Turnover:

Fixed Asset Turnover measures a company's efficiency in utilizing its fixed assets. We explore the art of using this ratio to evaluate asset productivity.

31. The Role of Debt Coverage Ratios:

Debt coverage ratios assess a company's ability to service its debt. We discuss the art of using debt coverage ratios to evaluate financial stability.

32. The Art of Interpreting EBITDA Margin:

EBITDA Margin measures a company's operating profitability. We explore the art of using EBITDA Margin to assess operational efficiency.

33. The Power of Operating Cash Flow Margin:

Operating Cash Flow Margin measures a company's cash-generating efficiency from operations. We discuss the art of using this margin to evaluate cash flow generation.

34. The Influence of Financial Leverage Ratios:

Financial leverage ratios assess the impact of debt on a company's earnings. We explore the art of using financial leverage ratios to understand the level of financial risk.

35. The Art of Using Price-Earnings-to-Growth (PEG) Ratio:

The PEG ratio factors in a company's growth rate relative to its P/E ratio. We discuss the art of using the PEG ratio to assess growth potential.

36. The Role of Dividend Payout Ratio:

Dividend Payout Ratio measures the proportion of earnings distributed as dividends. We discuss the art of using this ratio to evaluate a company's dividend policy and sustainability.

37. The Art of Analyzing Free Cash Flow (FCF):

Free Cash Flow represents cash available to investors after accounting for capital expenditures. We explore the art of using FCF to assess a company's ability to invest, repay debt, and pay dividends.

38. The Power of Earnings Before Interest, Taxes, Depreciation, and Amortization (EBITDA):

EBITDA is a measure of a company's operating performance. We discuss the art of using EBITDA to analyze profitability and compare companies with different capital structures.

39. The Influence of Return on Assets (ROA):

ROA measures a company's profitability relative to its total assets. We explore the art of using ROA to evaluate how efficiently a company uses its assets to generate profits.

40. The Art of Analyzing Return on Investment (ROI):

ROI assesses the return generated from an investment relative to its cost. We discuss the art of using ROI to evaluate the profitability of specific projects or investments.

41. The Role of Return on Equity (ROE) Dupont Analysis:

ROE DuPont Analysis breaks down ROE into its components. We explore the art of using this analysis to understand the factors driving a company's profitability.

42. The Art of Analyzing Working Capital Ratios:

Working capital ratios assess a company's short-term liquidity. We discuss the art of using these ratios to understand a company's ability to meet its short-term obligations.

43. The Power of Coverage Ratios:

Coverage ratios measure a company's ability to meet its obligations. We explore the art of using coverage ratios to assess the company's ability to service its debt and pay interest.

44. The Influence of Cash Conversion Cycle (CCC):

CCC measures the time it takes to convert resources into cash flows. We discuss the art of using CCC to evaluate a company's efficiency in managing its cash flow.

45. The Art of Analyzing Operating Margin:

Operating Margin measures a company's profitability from core business operations. We explore the art of using this margin to assess operating efficiency.

46. The Role of Gross Margin:

Gross Margin measures a company's profitability from producing goods or services. We discuss the art of using Gross Margin to evaluate cost management.

47. The Art of Analyzing Net Margin:

Net Margin measures a company's profitability after all expenses, including taxes and interest. We explore the art of using Net Margin to assess overall profitability.

48. The Power of Return on Investment Capital (ROIC):

ROIC measures the return generated from invested capital. We discuss the art of using ROIC to evaluate how effectively a company utilizes its invested capital.

49. The Influence of Price-to-Earnings Growth (PEG) Ratio:

PEG ratio considers a company's growth rate relative to its P/E ratio. We explore the art of using PEG ratio to assess whether a stock is overvalued or undervalued based on growth prospects.

50. The Art of Analyzing Financial Statement Footnotes:

Financial statement footnotes provide additional information and context. We discuss the art of reading and understanding footnotes to gain deeper insights into a company's financials.

Conclusion:

"The Art of Reading Financial Statements" celebrates the mastery of interpreting the financial data presented in company reports. Just as a skilled artist uses brushstrokes to bring a painting to life, investors can use their understanding of financial statements to uncover the true financial picture of a company. By embracing the art and science of financial statement analysis, investors can make informed decisions, identify potential risks and opportunities, and navigate the complexities of financial markets with greater confidence and precision.

In the tapestry of investment success, the art of reading financial statements becomes a brushstroke that adds depth, clarity, and insight to the investment journey. As investors seek to make prudent choices amidst the vast sea of financial information, the art of reading financial statements remains an essential skill that empowers them to identify solid investment prospects, assess financial health, and align their investment strategies with their financial goals.

As the investment landscape continues to evolve, the colors of financial statement analysis will remain an integral part of the investor's palette. By carefully curating an approach that combines financial acumen, critical thinking, and thorough analysis, investors can create financial masterpieces that reflect their vision, discipline, and ability to uncover the hidden nuances within financial statements. With this profound understanding, investors can confidently navigate the ever-changing currents of financial markets and make decisions that lead them towards their desired financial objectives.

CHAPTER 33: SCULPTING SUCCESS: LEARNING FROM FAILURES

Introduction:

In Chapter 33, "Sculpting Success: Learning from Failures," we embark on a profound journey that explores the invaluable lessons hidden within failures. Just as a skilled sculptor molds masterpieces by refining their work through trial and error, successful individuals in various fields have embraced failure as a stepping stone to greatness. This chapter delves into the art of embracing failure, understanding its role in personal and professional growth, and harnessing its transformative power to sculpt a path towards success.

1. The Nature of Failure:

Failure is an inevitable part of the human experience. We discuss the essence of failure and its significance in the journey towards success.

2. The Art of Embracing Failure:

Embracing failure requires a shift in perspective. We explore the art of accepting failure as a valuable teacher and a catalyst for growth.

3. The Power of Resilience:

Resilience is the ability to bounce back from setbacks. We discuss the art of cultivating resilience to navigate challenges and setbacks with determination.

4. The Influence of Growth Mindset:

A growth mindset fosters a belief in the potential for growth and improvement. We explore the art of adopting a growth mindset to view failures as opportunities for learning.

5. The Art of Learning from Mistakes:

Mistakes offer invaluable lessons. We discuss the art of analyzing mistakes to identify areas for improvement and prevent repeating them.

6. The Role of Self-Reflection:

Self-reflection fosters introspection and self-awareness. We explore the art of engaging in self-reflection to understand personal strengths and weaknesses.

7. The Art of Constructive Feedback:

Constructive feedback provides valuable insights. We discuss the art of seeking and accepting feedback to enhance personal and professional development.

8. The Power of Adaptability:

Adaptability enables individuals to thrive in changing circumstances. We explore the art of being adaptable to respond effectively to failure and uncertainty.

9. The Influence of Perseverance:

Perseverance is the determination to persist in the face of adversity. We discuss the art of cultivating perseverance to overcome challenges and achieve long-term goals.

10. The Art of Embracing Vulnerability:

Vulnerability allows for genuine connections and growth. We explore the art of embracing vulnerability as a means to learn from failures and connect with others.

11. The Role of Humility:

Humility involves acknowledging limitations and learning from others. We discuss the art of practicing humility to foster a receptive attitude towards failures.

12. The Art of Turning Setbacks into Comebacks:

Setbacks can lead to powerful comebacks. We explore the art of turning failures into opportunities for personal and professional growth.

13. The Power of Reinvention:

Reinvention involves adapting to change and evolving. We discuss the art of reinventing oneself to overcome failures and achieve new heights of success.

14. The Influence of Mindfulness:

Mindfulness cultivates present-moment awareness. We explore the art of practicing mindfulness to approach failures with clarity and composure.

15. The Art of Cultivating Patience:

Patience allows for gradual progress and learning. We discuss the art of cultivating patience to persist in the face of failures.

16. The Role of Emotional Intelligence:

Emotional intelligence helps manage emotions effectively. We explore the art of developing emotional intelligence to cope with failure and setbacks.

17. The Art of Turning Weaknesses into Strengths:

Failures can highlight areas for improvement. We discuss the art of transforming weaknesses into strengths through continuous learning and development.

18. The Power of Positive Thinking:

Positive thinking fosters optimism and resilience. We explore the art of adopting a positive mindset to navigate failures with a constructive outlook.

19. The Influence of Goal Setting:

Goal setting provides direction and motivation. We discuss the art of setting realistic and achievable goals to learn from failures and measure progress.

20. The Art of Surrounding Yourself with Supportive

Individuals:

A supportive network provides encouragement and perspective. We explore the art of surrounding oneself with supportive people who foster growth and learning.

21. The Role of Gratitude:

Gratitude fosters a sense of appreciation and resilience. We discuss the art of practicing gratitude to maintain perspective during challenging times.

22. The Art of Accepting Imperfection:

Accepting imperfection reduces self-imposed pressure. We explore the art of embracing imperfections as part of the journey towards success.

23. The Power of Visualization:

Visualization helps envision future success. We discuss the art of using visualization to focus on desired outcomes even amidst failures.

24. The Influence of Stoicism:

Stoicism promotes emotional resilience and wisdom. We explore the art of applying stoic principles to navigate failures with composure.

25. The Art of Learning from Role Models:

Role models offer inspiration and guidance. We discuss the art of learning from the experiences of successful individuals who have overcome failures.

26. The Role of Courage:

Courage is essential to embrace challenges. We explore the art of cultivating courage to face failures and take calculated risks.

27. The Art of Cultivating Creativity:

Creativity fosters innovative problem-solving. We discuss the art of harnessing creativity to find novel solutions to challenges posed by failures.

28. The Power of Self-Compassion:

Self-compassion involves treating oneself with kindness. We explore the art of practicing self-compassion to foster resilience in the face of failures.

29. The Influence of Time Management:

Effective time management maximizes productivity. We discuss the art of managing time efficiently to learn from failures and focus on personal growth.

30. The Art of Learning from the Journey:

The journey itself is a valuable teacher. We explore the art of embracing the learning process, even if it involves failures.

31. The Role of Mentorship:

Mentorship offers guidance and support. We discuss the art of seeking mentorship to gain wisdom from experienced individuals who have overcome failures.

32. The Art of Fostering a Growth-Oriented Culture:

A growth-oriented culture promotes learning and development. We explore the art of fostering such a culture in personal and professional environments.

33. The Power of Honesty:

Honesty fosters accountability and growth. We discuss the art of being honest with oneself and others about failures and areas for improvement.

Conclusion:

"Sculpting Success: Learning from Failures" celebrates the transformative power of failures in shaping individuals and propelling them towards success. Just as a skilled sculptor meticulously chips away at stone to reveal a masterpiece, individuals can sculpt their paths towards greatness by embracing failures and learning from them. By understanding that failures are stepping stones, not stumbling blocks, one can harness the wisdom gleaned from mistakes and setbacks to pave the way towards personal and professional growth.

In the tapestry of success, the art of learning from failures becomes the brushstroke that adds depth, resilience, and wisdom to the individual's journey. As individuals navigate through the ebb and flow of life, the art of learning from failures remains a guiding principle that empowers them to rise above challenges, uncover their true potential, and unlock their creative spirit.

As the journey of personal and professional growth continues, the colors of learning from failures will remain an integral part of the individual's palette. By carefully curating a mindset of curiosity, self-compassion, and resilience, individuals can sculpt their experiences into a mosaic of wisdom, courage, and humility. Through this profound process of self-discovery and refinement, individuals can transform their failures into stepping stones that lead them to success and fulfillment.

CHAPTER 34: THE ART OF RISK MANAGEMENT

Introduction:

In Chapter 34, "The Art of Risk Management," we delve into the critical discipline of identifying, assessing, and mitigating risks in various aspects of life and business. Just as a skilled artist carefully plans each stroke to create a masterpiece, effective risk management involves a systematic approach to anticipate potential threats and uncertainties. This chapter explores the importance of risk management, the art of risk assessment, and the strategies to safeguard against adverse events while capitalizing on opportunities.

1. The Nature of Risk:

Risk is an inherent part of all human endeavors. We discuss the essence of risk and its implications in decision-making and resource allocation.

2. The Art of Risk Perception:

Perception influences how individuals perceive and respond to risks. We explore the art of understanding risk perception to make informed decisions.

3. The Power of Risk Appetite and Tolerance:

Risk appetite reflects the willingness to take on risk for potential rewards. We discuss the art of aligning risk appetite with business objectives and individual preferences.

4. The Influence of Risk Assessment:

Risk assessment involves identifying and analyzing potential risks. We explore the art of conducting thorough risk assessments to understand their impact and likelihood.

5. The Art of Quantitative Risk Analysis:

Quantitative risk analysis involves assigning numerical values to risks. We discuss the art of using statistical models and data analysis to quantify risks.

6. The Role of Qualitative Risk Analysis:

Qualitative risk analysis involves subjective assessments of risks. We explore the art of using expert judgment and risk matrices to evaluate risks.

7. The Art of Risk Mapping:

Risk mapping visually represents the distribution of risks. We discuss the art of creating risk maps to prioritize risk management efforts.

8. The Power of Scenario Analysis:

Scenario analysis involves exploring different risk scenarios. We explore the art of using scenario analysis to prepare for a range of potential outcomes.

9. The Influence of Risk Registers:

Risk registers document identified risks and mitigation strategies. We discuss the art of maintaining comprehensive risk registers for effective risk tracking.

10. The Art of Risk Control:

Risk control involves implementing measures to reduce risks. We explore the art of selecting and implementing risk control strategies.

11. The Role of Risk Avoidance:

Risk avoidance involves eliminating activities with high potential for harm. We discuss the art of using risk avoidance to steer clear of undue risks.

12. The Art of Risk Transfer:

Risk transfer involves shifting risks to other parties through insurance or contracts. We explore the art of using risk transfer to protect against financial losses.

13. The Power of Risk Reduction:

Risk reduction involves implementing measures to decrease the likelihood or impact of risks. We discuss the art of using risk reduction strategies to minimize exposure.

14. The Influence of Risk Mitigation:

Risk mitigation involves taking action to reduce risks' consequences. We explore the art of applying risk mitigation techniques to lessen potential harm.

15. The Art of Risk Retention:

Risk retention involves accepting and managing risks internally. We discuss the art of retaining risks when the costs of avoidance or transfer outweigh potential benefits.

16. The Role of Risk Sharing:

Risk sharing involves distributing risks among multiple parties. We explore the art of using risk-sharing mechanisms like partnerships and joint ventures.

17. The Art of Risk Monitoring:

Risk monitoring involves continuously assessing risks and their impact. We discuss the art of establishing robust risk monitoring systems.

18. The Power of Early Warning Systems:

Early warning systems detect potential risks in advance. We explore the art of using early warning systems to take proactive measures.

19. The Influence of Risk Reporting:

Risk reporting communicates risks to stakeholders. We discuss the art of creating concise and transparent risk reports.

20. The Art of Risk Communication:

Risk communication involves conveying risk information

effectively. We explore the art of clear and timely risk communication.

21. The Role of Risk Governance:

Risk governance establishes the framework for risk management. We discuss the art of developing effective risk governance structures.

22. The Art of Enterprise Risk Management (ERM):

ERM involves comprehensive risk management across an organization. We explore the art of integrating risk management into strategic planning.

23. The Power of Operational Risk Management:

Operational risk management focuses on risks related to processes and systems. We discuss the art of enhancing operational risk management to improve efficiency.

24. The Influence of Financial Risk Management:

Financial risk management addresses risks related to financial instruments and markets. We explore the art of using financial risk management tools like hedging.

25. The Art of Market Risk Management:

Market risk management addresses risks arising from market fluctuations. We discuss the art of using diversification and hedging to manage market risks.

26. The Role of Credit Risk Management:

Credit risk management addresses risks of default on credit obligations. We explore the art of using credit analysis and risk pricing to manage credit risks.

27. The Art of Liquidity Risk Management:

Liquidity risk management ensures sufficient cash to meet obligations. We discuss the art of maintaining liquidity reserves and contingency plans.

28. The Power of Interest Rate Risk Management:

Interest rate risk management addresses risks from interest rate fluctuations. We explore the art of using interest rate derivatives to manage these risks.

29. The Influence of Reputational Risk Management:

Reputational risk management safeguards a company's image. We discuss the art of building a strong reputation and crisis management.

30. The Art of Regulatory Risk Management:

Regulatory risk management ensures compliance with laws and regulations. We explore the art of staying updated on regulations and implementing necessary changes.

31. The Role of Technology in Risk Management:

Technology enhances risk management processes. We discuss the art of using advanced analytics and risk management software.

32. The Art of Environmental, Social, and Governance (ESG) Risk Management:

ESG risk management addresses non-financial risks. We explore the art of integrating ESG considerations into risk assessments.

33. The Power of Cybersecurity Risk Management:

Cybersecurity risk management protects against data breaches and cyber-attacks. We discuss the art of implementing robust cybersecurity measures.

34. The Influence of Supply Chain Risk Management:

Supply chain risk management addresses vulnerabilities in supply chains. We explore the art of diversifying suppliers and contingency planning.

35. The Art of Strategic Risk Management:

Strategic risk management addresses risks that impact strategic objectives. We discuss the art of aligning risk management with business strategy.

36. The Role of Crisis Management:

Crisis management addresses risks of major disruptions. We explore the art of developing crisis response plans.

37. The Art of Project Risk Management:

Project risk management addresses risks in project execution. We discuss the art of risk identification and mitigation in project management.

38. The Power of Country and Political Risk Management:

Country and political risk management assess risks in international operations. We explore the art of political risk analysis and hedging.

39. The Influence of Natural and Environmental Risk Management:

Natural and environmental risk management addresses natural disasters and climate-related risks. We discuss the art of conducting risk assessments for environmental hazards and implementing measures to enhance resilience.

40. The Art of Supply Chain Resilience:

Supply chain resilience involves preparing for disruptions in the supply chain. We explore the art of diversifying suppliers, building redundancy, and enhancing supply chain visibility.

41. The Role of Reputation Risk Management:

Reputation risk management safeguards against damage to a company's reputation. We discuss the art of maintaining a positive image and responding to crises effectively.

42. The Power of Fraud Risk Management:

Fraud risk management addresses the risk of financial fraud. We explore the art of implementing internal controls and fraud detection mechanisms.

43. The Influence of Geopolitical Risk Management:

Geopolitical risk management assesses risks arising from

geopolitical events. We discuss the art of staying informed about global events and their potential impact.

44. The Art of Insurance and Risk Transfer:

Insurance and risk transfer involve transferring risks to insurance providers. We explore the art of selecting appropriate insurance coverage and negotiating favorable terms.

45. The Role of Risk Culture:

Risk culture refers to the collective attitudes and behaviors towards risk within an organization. We discuss the art of fostering a risk-aware and responsible culture.

46. The Power of Risk Leadership:

Risk leadership involves setting the tone for risk management at the highest levels of an organization. We explore the art of effective risk leadership and governance.

47. The Influence of Behavioral Risk Management:

Behavioral risk management addresses the impact of human behavior on risk-taking. We discuss the art of recognizing cognitive biases and their influence on decision-making.

48. The Art of Stress Testing:

Stress testing involves subjecting systems to extreme scenarios to assess their resilience. We explore the art of conducting stress tests to understand potential vulnerabilities.

49. The Role of Risk Communication in Crisis:

Risk communication is crucial during crises. We discuss the art of clear and transparent communication to manage expectations and mitigate panic.

50. The Art of Learning from Risk Events:

Learning from risk events is vital for continuous improvement. We explore the art of conducting post-mortems and incorporating lessons into risk management processes.

Conclusion:

"The Art of Risk Management" celebrates the profound impact of effective risk management in steering individuals and organizations towards success. Just as a skilled artist carefully crafts a masterpiece by considering every detail, risk management involves a meticulous approach to anticipate and address potential risks. By embracing the art and science of risk management, individuals and businesses can protect their interests, capitalize on opportunities, and navigate the ever-changing landscape of uncertainty with resilience and confidence.

In the tapestry of achievement, the art of risk management becomes a brushstroke that adds depth, security, and foresight to the path of progress. As individuals and organizations embark on ambitious endeavors, the art of risk management remains an indispensable skill that enables them to make informed decisions, safeguard against potential pitfalls, and optimize their chances of success.

As the world continues to evolve, the colors of risk management will remain an integral part of the palette of progress. By carefully curating an approach that combines risk awareness, adaptability, and innovation, individuals and organizations can sculpt their destinies amidst the dynamic and unpredictable landscape of life and business. Through this profound understanding and application of risk management principles, they can confidently navigate uncharted waters, embrace opportunities, and flourish in the face of uncertainty.

CHAPTER 35: EMBRACING ARTISTIC INTUITION IN INVESTING

Introduction:

In Chapter 35, "Embracing Artistic Intuition in Investing," we explore the intriguing concept of using artistic intuition as a valuable tool in the investment decision-making process. Just as a skilled artist relies on intuition to create captivating masterpieces, successful investors can harness their intuitive abilities to make informed and insightful investment choices. This chapter delves into the connection between artistry and investing, the art of tapping into one's intuition, and the strategies to combine analytical thinking with intuitive insights to achieve investment success.

1. The Intersection of Art and Investing:

Art and investing are both forms of creative expression. We discuss the intriguing parallels between the artistic process and the investment journey.

2. The Essence of Intuition:

Intuition is the ability to understand or know something without conscious reasoning. We explore the nature of intuition and its role in human decision-making.

3. The Art of Cultivating Intuition:

Cultivating intuition involves honing one's self-awareness and sensitivity to subtle cues. We discuss the art of developing intuition as an investment skill.

4. The Power of Gut Feelings in Investing:

Gut feelings are instinctive reactions to investment

opportunities. We explore the art of trusting and interpreting gut feelings when making investment choices.

5. The Influence of Emotional Intelligence:

Emotional intelligence helps in understanding and managing emotions. We discuss the art of using emotional intelligence to harness intuitive insights effectively.

6. The Art of Listening to Market Sentiment:

Market sentiment reflects the prevailing mood of investors. We explore the art of interpreting market sentiment through intuition.

7. The Role of Pattern Recognition:

Pattern recognition enables investors to identify trends and opportunities. We discuss the art of using intuition to recognize meaningful patterns in market data.

8. The Art of Reading between the Lines:

Reading between the lines involves understanding subtle signals and hidden meanings. We explore the art of using intuition to uncover valuable insights from financial information.

9. The Power of Visualization in Investing:

Visualization allows investors to mentally project potential outcomes. We discuss the art of using intuitive visualization to envision investment scenarios.

10. The Influence of Instinctual Decision-making:

Instinctual decision-making relies on rapid and subconscious processing. We explore the art of combining instinct with analysis to make sound investment choices.

11. The Art of Trusting Unconventional Insights:

Unconventional insights may challenge conventional wisdom. We discuss the art of trusting and exploring unconventional investment ideas driven by intuition.

THE ART OF PROFIT

12. The Role of Cognitive Biases in Intuition:

Cognitive biases can influence intuitive judgments. We explore the art of recognizing and mitigating biases to improve intuitive decision-making.

13. The Art of Mindful Investing:

Mindful investing involves staying present and aware during investment decisions. We discuss the art of using mindfulness to enhance intuitive judgment.

14. The Power of Serendipity in Investing:

Serendipity involves discovering valuable insights by chance. We explore the art of being open to serendipitous moments in the investment process.

15. The Influence of Artistic Inspiration:

Artistic inspiration can spark creativity and innovative thinking. We discuss the art of drawing inspiration from diverse sources in the investment world.

16. The Art of Deciphering Market Signals:

Market signals offer hints about future trends. We explore the art of intuitively deciphering market signals to make timely investment moves.

17. The Role of Intuition in Risk Management:

Intuition can guide risk management decisions. We discuss the art of using intuitive insights to assess and manage investment risks.

18. The Art of Timing in Investing:

Timing is critical in seizing opportunities. We explore the art of using intuition to make well-timed investment decisions.

19. The Power of Patience and Intuition:

Patience allows for intuitive insights to mature. We discuss the art of combining patience with intuition in long-term investment strategies.

20. The Influence of Mind-Body Connection in Intuition:

The mind-body connection can influence intuitive perception. We explore the art of maintaining physical and mental well-being to enhance intuition.

21. The Art of Analyzing Behavioral Patterns:

Behavioral patterns offer insights into investor behavior. We discuss the art of using intuition to analyze and anticipate market behavior.

22. The Role of Meditation in Developing Intuition:

Meditation enhances self-awareness and focus. We explore the art of using meditation to cultivate a deeper connection with intuitive insights.

23. The Art of Embracing Ambiguity in Investing:

Ambiguity is inherent in investment decisions. We discuss the art of using intuition to navigate uncertainty and ambiguity.

24. The Power of Collective Intuition:

Collective intuition refers to shared intuitive insights among a group. We explore the art of harnessing collective intuition in investment forums.

25. The Influence of Intuition in Contrarian Investing:

Contrarian investing involves going against prevailing market sentiment. We discuss the art of using intuition to identify contrarian opportunities.

26. The Art of Intuitive Portfolio Management:

Intuitive portfolio management involves dynamic adjustments based on intuition. We explore the art of using intuition to optimize investment portfolios.

27. The Role of Dreams and Intuition in Investing:

Dreams can offer subconscious insights. We discuss the art of interpreting dreams to gain investment wisdom.

28. The Art of Intuitive Due Diligence:

Intuitive due diligence complements analytical research. We explore the art of using intuition to assess investment opportunities.

29. The Power of Flexibility in Intuitive Investing:

Flexibility allows investors to adapt to changing conditions. We discuss the art of using intuition to make flexible investment decisions.

30. The Influence of Past Experiences on Intuition:

Past experiences shape intuitive judgment. We explore the art of using lessons from the past to inform current investment decisions.

31. The Art of Intuitive Exit Strategies:

Intuitive exit strategies involve reading market signals to time exits. We discuss the art of using intuition to exit investments at the right moment.

32. The Role of Intuition in Identifying Market Trends:

Intuition can guide investors in identifying emerging trends. We explore the art of using intuition to capitalize on market shifts.

33. The Art of Intuitive Position Sizing:

Intuitive position sizing involves adjusting investments based on intuition. We discuss the art of using intuition to determine optimal position sizes.

34. The Power of Intuition in Entrepreneurial Investing:

Entrepreneurial investing requires bold decision-making. We explore the art of using intuition in entrepreneurial investment ventures.

35. The Influence of Intuition in Socially Responsible Investing:

Intuition can align with values in socially responsible investing. We discuss the art of using intuition to make ethical investment choices.

Conclusion:

"Embracing Artistic Intuition in Investing" celebrates the transformative potential of intuitive insights in the complex world of finance and investments. Just as an artist's intuition guides the creation of an extraordinary masterpiece, intuitive insights can lead investors to extraordinary investment opportunities and outcomes. By embracing the art and science of tapping into one's intuition, investors can gain a deeper understanding of market dynamics, identify hidden opportunities, and make bold decisions that drive them towards investment success.

In the tapestry of investment achievement, the art of embracing artistic intuition becomes a brushstroke that adds depth, creativity, and innovation to the canvas of investment strategy. As investors navigate the ever-changing landscape of financial markets, the art of embracing intuitive insights remains an essential skill that empowers them to navigate uncertainties, uncover unique investment prospects, and achieve their financial objectives with a sense of purpose and foresight.

CHAPTER 36: INVESTING IN THE GIG ECONOMY: THE RISE OF FREELANCERS

Introduction:

In Chapter 36, "Investing in the Gig Economy: The Rise of Freelancers," we explore the revolutionary shift in the workforce landscape, where traditional employment models are gradually giving way to the rise of freelancers and independent contractors. The gig economy has emerged as a powerful economic force, reshaping the way people work, companies operate, and investors approach investment opportunities. This chapter delves into the gig economy's growth, the impact on various industries, the art of identifying lucrative investment avenues, and the strategies to capitalize on this dynamic and transformative economic trend.

1. The Gig Economy: A Paradigm Shift in Work:

The gig economy refers to a labor market characterized by short-term contracts and freelance work. We discuss the evolution of the gig economy and its impact on the traditional employment landscape.

2. The Essence of Freelancing:

Freelancers are independent workers who offer their services to multiple clients. We explore the motivations behind choosing freelancing as a career path.

3. The Gig Economy's Growth Drivers:

Several factors contribute to the rapid growth of the gig economy. We discuss technological advancements, changing workforce preferences, and business model innovations.

4. The Art of Spotting Gig Economy Trends:

Identifying gig economy trends is crucial for investment decision-making. We explore the art of recognizing emerging trends and disruptions in the gig economy.

5. The Power of Platforms:

Technology platforms connect freelancers with clients. We discuss the role of gig economy platforms and their impact on the investment landscape.

6. The Gig Economy's Impact on Industries:

The gig economy has transformed various industries. We explore how sectors such as transportation, e-commerce, and healthcare have adapted to gig economy dynamics.

7. The Art of Understanding Labor Laws:

Labor laws play a vital role in gig economy regulations. We discuss the challenges and implications of evolving labor laws on gig economy investments.

8. The Influence of Remote Work:

Remote work has become a cornerstone of the gig economy. We explore the art of investing in companies that enable and benefit from remote work trends.

9. The Gig Economy and Entrepreneurship:

The gig economy has fostered entrepreneurship. We discuss the art of investing in startups and platforms that support gig economy entrepreneurs.

10. The Role of Skills Training and Upskilling:

Skills training is essential for gig economy success. We explore the art of investing in education and training platforms that cater to gig economy workers.

11. The Art of Investing in Freelancer Platforms:

Freelancer platforms present investment opportunities. We discuss the key considerations when evaluating and investing in gig economy platforms.

12. The Power of On-Demand Services:

On-demand services are a significant gig economy segment. We explore the art of investing in companies offering on-demand solutions.

13. The Gig Economy's Impact on Traditional Business Models:

Traditional businesses are adapting to the gig economy's rise. We discuss the art of investing in companies that embrace gig economy principles.

14. The Influence of the Sharing Economy:

The sharing economy is closely related to the gig economy. We explore investment opportunities in the sharing economy ecosystem.

15. The Art of Investing in Gig Workers' Well-being:

Freelancers' well-being impacts productivity and job satisfaction. We discuss the art of investing in companies addressing gig workers' needs.

16. The Role of Digital Payment Solutions:

Digital payment solutions are essential in the gig economy. We explore the art of investing in fintech companies driving digital payments in gig work.

17. The Art of Diversification in Gig Economy Investments:

Diversification is vital in gig economy investing. We discuss the art of building a diversified portfolio to manage risk in this evolving market.

18. The Power of Blockchain in the Gig Economy:

Blockchain technology can enhance gig economy transactions. We explore the art of investing in blockchain projects transforming the gig economy.

19. The Gig Economy's Impact on Real Estate:

The gig economy influences housing and workspace demands. We discuss investment opportunities in real estate sectors affected by the gig economy.

20. The Influence of the Remote Work Revolution:

The gig economy fuels the remote work revolution. We explore the art of investing in companies enabling remote work arrangements.

21. The Art of Evaluating Gig Economy Startups:

Startups drive innovation in the gig economy. We discuss the art of assessing and investing in early-stage gig economy ventures.

22. The Role of Artificial Intelligence in Gig Economy Platforms:

Artificial intelligence enhances gig economy platforms. We explore the art of investing in AI-driven gig economy solutions.

23. The Art of Investing in Freelancer Benefits:

Freelancers seek benefits like healthcare and retirement options. We discuss the art of investing in companies providing gig workers with essential benefits.

24. The Power of Gig Economy Marketplaces:

Gig economy marketplaces connect freelancers with clients. We explore investment opportunities in successful gig economy marketplaces.

25. The Gig Economy and Financial Services:

Financial services play a vital role in gig economy ecosystems. We discuss the art of investing in fintech companies catering to gig economy workers.

26. The Art of Evaluating Gig Economy Risk Factors:

Gig economy investments come with unique risks. We explore the art of analyzing risk factors in gig economy ventures.

27. The Role of Gig Economy Regulation:

Regulation affects the gig economy's growth and stability. We discuss the art of navigating regulatory landscapes in gig economy investments.

28. The Art of Investing in Gig Economy Marketing:

Marketing is crucial for gig economy platforms' success. We explore investment opportunities in gig economy marketing solutions.

29. The Influence of Gig Economy Workforce Demographics:

Understanding gig economy workforce demographics informs investments. We discuss the art of targeting specific demographics in the gig economy.

30. The Gig Economy's Impact on Supply Chains:

The gig economy affects supply chain management. We explore investment opportunities in companies adapting to gig economy-driven supply chains.

31. The Role of Gig Economy Data Analytics:

Data analytics drives gig economy insights. We discuss the art of investing in companies leveraging data analytics in the gig economy.

32. The Art of Identifying Disruptive Gig Economy Startups:

Disruptive startups can revolutionize the gig economy. We explore the art of identifying and investing in innovative gig economy ventures.

33. The Power of Gig Economy Research and Market Analysis:

Market research informs gig economy investments. We discuss the art of conducting thorough research for gig economy investment decisions.

34. The Gig Economy's Impact on Work-Life Balance:

Work-life balance is crucial for gig workers' satisfaction. We explore the art of investing in companies promoting work-life balance in the gig economy.

35. The Art of Identifying Gig Economy Investment Risks and Rewards:

Gig economy investments come with unique opportunities and challenges. We discuss the art of balancing risk and reward in gig economy investments.

Conclusion:

"Investing in the Gig Economy: The Rise of Freelancers" celebrates the transformative potential of gig economy investments in an increasingly dynamic and agile world of work. Just as the gig economy revolutionizes the traditional employment landscape, savvy investors can capitalize on this economic shift by identifying lucrative investment avenues and leveraging disruptive trends in the gig economy. By embracing the art and science of gig economy investing, individuals and businesses can position themselves for growth and success in a rapidly evolving economic landscape.

CHAPTER 37: THE ART OF INVESTMENT RESEARCH

Introduction:

In Chapter 37, "The Art of Investment Research," we delve into the foundational aspect of successful investing - research. Just as an artist spends countless hours perfecting their craft, investors must diligently conduct comprehensive research to make informed decisions. This chapter explores the art of investment research, the various types of research methods, the importance of data analysis, and the strategies to translate research insights into profitable investment strategies.

1. The Significance of Investment Research:

Investment research is the bedrock of successful decision-making in the financial markets. We discuss how research empowers investors to navigate complexities and mitigate risks.

2. The Art of Setting Investment Objectives:

Setting clear investment objectives is the first step in the research process. We explore how defining objectives helps in guiding research efforts effectively.

3. The Influence of Economic Analysis:

Economic analysis examines macroeconomic factors impacting investments. We discuss the art of interpreting economic indicators and their relevance to investment decisions.

4. The Art of Fundamental Analysis:

Fundamental analysis evaluates a company's financial health and growth potential. We explore the art of analyzing financial statements and key performance indicators.

5. The Power of Technical Analysis:

Technical analysis studies historical price and volume data to forecast future price movements. We discuss the art of using charts and patterns to make trading decisions.

6. The Art of Sector and Industry Analysis:

Sector and industry analysis focus on specific segments of the market. We explore the art of identifying promising sectors and assessing their growth prospects.

7. The Influence of Company Valuation:

Valuation methods determine a company's intrinsic worth. We discuss the art of using valuation ratios and models to estimate fair value.

8. The Art of Conducting Market Research:

Market research examines customer behavior and market trends. We explore the art of conducting market surveys and analyzing consumer preferences.

9. The Power of Competitor Analysis:

Competitor analysis evaluates a company's rivals. We discuss the art of understanding competitive advantages and positioning in the market.

10. The Art of Analyzing Management and Leadership:

Management quality affects a company's performance. We explore the art of assessing leadership capabilities and corporate governance practices.

11. The Influence of Environmental, Social, and Governance (ESG) Research:

ESG research evaluates a company's impact on society and the environment. We discuss the art of incorporating ESG factors into investment decisions.

12. The Art of Understanding Industry Trends:

Industry trends shape investment opportunities. We explore the art of researching emerging trends and disruptive technologies.

13. The Power of Macro Trend Analysis:

Macro trend analysis examines long-term economic and societal shifts. We discuss the art of identifying investment themes aligned with macro trends.

14. The Art of Using Data Analytics:

Data analytics extracts insights from large datasets. We explore the art of leveraging data analytics to gain a competitive edge in investing.

15. The Influence of Sentiment Analysis:

Sentiment analysis gauges market sentiment and investor emotions. We discuss the art of incorporating sentiment analysis into investment research.

16. The Art of Reading Financial News and Reports:

Financial news and reports provide critical market updates. We explore the art of interpreting news and distinguishing credible sources.

17. The Power of Historical Performance Analysis:

Historical performance analysis assesses past investment results. We discuss the art of learning from history to inform future decisions.

18. The Art of Understanding Risk and Uncertainty:

Research must account for risk and uncertainty. We explore the art of risk analysis and scenario planning in investment research.

19. The Influence of Geopolitical Research:

Geopolitical events impact global markets. We discuss the art of analyzing geopolitical risks and their implications on investments.

20. The Art of Incorporating Behavioral Finance:

Behavioral finance studies how emotions influence investment decisions. We explore the art of understanding biases and their effects on research.

21. The Power of Qualitative Research:

Qualitative research involves subjective assessments. We discuss the art of conducting interviews and surveys to gain qualitative insights.

22. The Art of Quantitative Research:

Quantitative research involves numerical data and statistical analysis. We explore the art of using quantitative methods to draw objective conclusions.

23. The Influence of Academic Research:

Academic research contributes to investment knowledge. We discuss the art of referencing credible academic studies in investment decisions.

24. The Art of Building and Testing Investment Hypotheses:

Investment hypotheses guide research efforts. We explore the art of formulating and testing hypotheses to validate investment ideas.

25. The Power of Forecasting Models:

Forecasting models predict future performance. We discuss the art of using various forecasting techniques to anticipate market movements.

26. The Art of Identifying Industry Leaders:

Industry leaders often outperform competitors. We explore the art of identifying and investing in companies with a competitive edge.

27. The Influence of Industry Regulation and Government Policies:

Regulation and policies impact industries and sectors. We discuss the art of assessing regulatory risks and opportunities in investment research.

28. The Art of Scanning Financial Markets:

Financial markets offer vast opportunities. We explore the art of scanning markets to uncover potential investments.

29. The Art of Technical Indicator Analysis:

Technical indicators help in market timing. We discuss the art of using technical analysis tools to make entry and exit decisions.

30. The Influence of Central Bank Policies:

Central bank policies influence economic conditions. We explore the art of researching central bank actions and their impact on investments.

31. The Art of Industry Expertise:

Industry expertise enhances research insights. We discuss the art of seeking input from experts and insiders in specific sectors.

32. The Power of Contrarian Research:

Contrarian research challenges prevailing opinions. We explore the art of considering contrarian viewpoints in investment analysis.

33. The Art of Evaluating Risks and Returns:

Risk-return analysis guides investment choices. We discuss the art of balancing risk and reward in portfolio construction.

34. The Influence of Financial Market News:

Financial news impacts investor sentiment. We explore the art of interpreting news and avoiding knee-jerk reactions in investment decisions.

35. The Art of Identifying Long-term Trends:

Long-term trends shape investment strategies. We discuss the art of identifying and investing in trends with lasting potential.

36. The Power of Using Investment Screeners:

Investment screeners filter stocks based on specific criteria. We explore the art of using screeners to streamline research efforts.

37. The Art of Integrating Research into Investment Strategies:

Research insights inform investment strategies. We discuss the art of translating research findings into actionable investment decisions.

38. The Influence of Economic Forecasting:

Economic forecasting predicts economic performance. We explore the art of using economic forecasts to inform investment planning.

39. The Art of Analyzing Financial Models:

Financial models provide projections of future performance. We discuss the art of critically evaluating financial models for investment decisions.

40. The Art of Scenario Planning:

Scenario planning prepares for various outcomes. We explore the art of using scenario analysis to assess investment risks and rewards.

41. The Influence of Market Sentiment Analysis:

Market sentiment affects asset prices. We discuss the art of incorporating sentiment analysis into investment research.

42. The Art of Conducting Due Diligence:

Due diligence verifies investment opportunities. We explore the art of conducting thorough due diligence to minimize risks.

43. The Power of Earnings and Revenue Analysis:

Earnings and revenue growth drive stock performance. We discuss the art of analyzing financial metrics to identify promising investments.

44. The Art of Evaluating Dividend Stocks:

Dividend stocks offer income and potential for growth. We explore the art of analyzing dividend history and financial stability in dividend-paying companies.

45. The Influence of Interest Rates:

Interest rates impact various investment asset classes. We discuss the art of considering interest rate trends in investment decision-making.

46. The Art of Sector Rotation:

Sector rotation involves shifting investments based on market trends. We explore the art of strategically rotating investments across sectors to optimize returns.

47. The Power of Global Market Analysis:

Global markets are interconnected. We discuss the art of analyzing international trends and their influence on local investments.

48. The Art of Monitoring Market Volatility:

Market volatility affects investment performance. We explore the art of assessing and managing portfolio risks during volatile market conditions.

49. The Influence of Market Liquidity:

Market liquidity affects trade execution and asset prices. We discuss the art of evaluating liquidity factors in investment research.

50. The Art of Identifying Investment Themes:

Investment themes represent long-term opportunities. We explore the art of identifying and investing in themes that align with research insights.

51. The Role of Artificial Intelligence in Investment Research:

Artificial intelligence enhances research capabilities. We discuss the art of leveraging AI-powered tools for data analysis and investment decision-making.

52. The Art of Evaluating Management's Vision:

Management vision impacts a company's direction. We explore

the art of assessing management's strategic plans and execution capabilities.

53. The Power of Monitoring Regulatory Changes:

Regulatory changes influence investment landscapes. We discuss the art of staying informed about evolving regulations and their implications on investments.

54. The Art of Quantifying Risk and Reward:

Quantifying risk and reward aids in portfolio construction. We explore the art of using risk metrics and performance indicators in investment analysis.

55. The Influence of Environmental Analysis:

Environmental analysis examines factors like climate change and sustainability. We discuss the art of incorporating environmental considerations into investment decisions.

56. The Art of Identifying Value Stocks:

Value stocks are undervalued compared to their intrinsic worth. We explore the art of using valuation techniques to identify attractive value investments.

57. The Role of Industry Conferences and Events:

Industry events offer valuable insights and networking opportunities. We discuss the art of attending conferences for investment research purposes.

58. The Art of Evaluating Corporate Governance:

Strong corporate governance enhances company performance. We explore the art of analyzing governance practices in investment research.

59. The Power of Identifying Market Mispricing:

Market mispricing create investment opportunities. We discuss the art of spotting undervalued assets and potential arbitrage opportunities.

60. The Art of Analyzing Economic Indicators:

Economic indicators gauge economic health. We explore the art of interpreting economic data to make informed investment decisions.

Conclusion:

"The Art of Investment Research" celebrates the profound impact of thorough and thoughtful research in shaping successful investment strategies. Just as an artist hones their skills to create timeless masterpieces, investors must continuously refine their research techniques to navigate dynamic financial markets and seize lucrative opportunities. By embracing the art and science of investment research, individuals and institutions can make informed choices, mitigate risks, and achieve their financial goals with confidence and precision.

In the tapestry of investment excellence, the art of investment research becomes a brushstroke that adds depth, insight, and foresight to the canvas of financial success. As investors navigate the ever-changing landscape of opportunities and challenges, the art of conducting comprehensive research remains an indispensable skill that empowers them to make well-informed decisions, adapt to market dynamics, and create portfolios that stand the test of time. Through this profound understanding and application of research principles, investors can confidently paint their financial futures with colors of prosperity and resilience.

CHAPTER 38: THE WISDOM OF MARKET VETERANS

Introduction:

In Chapter 38, "The Wisdom of Market Veterans," we embark on a journey to learn from the seasoned experts and veterans of the financial markets. These market veterans have weathered numerous market cycles, experienced both triumphs and setbacks, and accumulated invaluable knowledge and insights along the way. This chapter celebrates the wisdom of these veterans, their time-tested strategies, and the lessons they can impart to investors seeking to navigate the complexities of the financial world.

1. The Significance of Market Veterans:

Market veterans are individuals with decades of experience in the financial industry. We discuss the value of their wisdom and how it can guide investors.

2. The Art of Learning from History:

Market veterans have witnessed historical market events. We explore the art of learning from past market cycles to inform present and future decisions.

3. The Influence of Long-Term Thinking:

Market veterans often emphasize the importance of a long-term investment horizon. We discuss the art of adopting a patient and disciplined approach to investing.

4. The Power of Emotional Discipline:

Market veterans have learned to manage emotions during market fluctuations. We explore the art of maintaining emotional discipline to avoid impulsive decisions.

5. The Art of Capital Preservation:

Preserving capital is a key focus for market veterans. We discuss the art of protecting investments from excessive risk and potential losses.

6. The Influence of Asset Allocation:

Asset allocation is a cornerstone of investment success. We explore the art of diversifying across asset classes to achieve optimal risk-adjusted returns.

7. The Art of Contrarian Thinking:

Market veterans often embrace contrarian perspectives. We discuss the art of seeking opportunities when market sentiment deviates from fundamentals.

8. The Power of Fundamental Analysis:

Fundamental analysis is a staple of market veterans' research process. We explore the art of evaluating the intrinsic value of investments.

9. The Art of Patience and Timing:

Market veterans understand the significance of timing in investing. We discuss the art of patiently waiting for the right investment opportunities.

10. The Influence of Market Cycles:

Market veterans have witnessed multiple market cycles. We explore the art of understanding and navigating through different market phases.

11. The Art of Risk Management:

Market veterans prioritize risk management. We discuss the art of employing risk mitigation strategies to protect portfolios.

12. The Power of Learning from Mistakes:

Market veterans have experienced both successes and failures. We explore the art of learning from investment mistakes and improving future decisions.

13. The Art of Staying Informed:

Market veterans emphasize the importance of staying informed about market developments. We discuss the art of conducting continuous research and analysis.

14. The Influence of Investment Philosophy:

Market veterans often adhere to a specific investment philosophy. We explore the art of aligning one's investment approach with personal beliefs and values.

15. The Art of Adapting to Change:

Market veterans have navigated through dynamic market environments. We discuss the art of adapting to changing economic and industry landscapes.

16. The Role of Mentorship:

Market veterans can serve as mentors to the next generation of investors. We explore the art of seeking mentorship and guidance in the investment journey.

17. The Art of Selective Investing:

Market veterans are discerning in their investment choices. We discuss the art of conducting thorough due diligence before making investment decisions.

18. The Influence of Market Sentiment:

Market veterans understand the impact of sentiment on asset prices. We explore the art of assessing market sentiment and its implications on investments.

19. The Art of Asset Preservation:

Market veterans prioritize preserving wealth for future generations. We discuss the art of estate planning and asset protection.

20. The Power of Financial Education:

Market veterans emphasize the value of financial literacy. We explore the art of continuous learning and improving investment knowledge.

21. The Art of Resilience:

Market veterans have endured market downturns and setbacks. We discuss the art of building resilience to navigate challenging market conditions.

22. The Influence of Global Events:

Market veterans have witnessed the impact of global events on financial markets. We explore the art of analyzing geopolitical and economic events.

23. The Art of Optimizing Tax Efficiency:

Market veterans consider tax implications in investment strategies. We discuss the art of optimizing tax efficiency to maximize after-tax returns.

24. The Power of Staying Grounded:

Market veterans avoid getting caught up in market hype. We explore the art of staying grounded and avoiding herd behavior.

25. The Art of Balancing Active and Passive Investing:

Market veterans may employ both active and passive investment approaches. We discuss the art of striking a balance between the two.

26. The Influence of Economic Indicators:

Market veterans closely monitor economic indicators. We explore the art of interpreting economic data to inform investment decisions.

27. The Art of Taking a Holistic View:

Market veterans consider multiple factors in their analysis. We discuss the art of taking a holistic view of investments and their broader impact.

28. The Power of Learning from Peers:

Market veterans collaborate with peers and industry

professionals. We explore the art of networking and learning from other investors.

29. The Art of Gratitude:

Market veterans appreciate the opportunities and challenges of the investment journey. We discuss the art of cultivating gratitude in investing.

30. The Influence of Sustainable Investing:

Market veterans consider the long-term impact of investments on society and the environment. We explore the art of integrating sustainable investing principles.

Conclusion:

"The Wisdom of Market Veterans" celebrates the invaluable insights and experiences of those who have navigated the financial markets over many decades. Just as a seasoned artist refines their craft through years of practice and dedication, market veterans have honed their investment skills through years of exposure to various market conditions and cycles. By embracing the art of learning from these wise veterans, investors can gain a deeper understanding of the intricacies of investing, avoid common pitfalls, and build portfolios that withstand the test of time.

In the tapestry of investment wisdom, the art of drawing from the experiences of market veterans becomes a brushstroke that adds depth, knowledge, and prudence to the canvas of financial success. As investors seek to navigate the ever-changing landscape of the financial markets, the wisdom of market veterans serves as a guiding light, illuminating the path to informed decision-making, sound risk management, and ultimately, prosperous and fulfilling investment journeys. Through the embrace of this profound wisdom, investors can confidently and artfully paint their financial futures with colors of prosperity and wisdom.

CHAPTER 39: THE ART OF ETHICAL INVESTING

Introduction:

In Chapter 39, "The Art of Ethical Investing," we explore the transformative approach of aligning investment decisions with personal values and ethical principles. Ethical investing, also known as socially responsible investing (SRI) or sustainable investing, has gained significant momentum as investors seek to make a positive impact on society and the environment. This chapter delves into the principles of ethical investing, the different strategies employed, the integration of environmental, social, and governance (ESG) factors, and the profound influence of ethical investing on the financial landscape.

1. The Significance of Ethical Investing:

Ethical investing seeks to generate positive outcomes beyond financial returns. We discuss the importance of aligning investments with personal values and societal goals.

2. The Art of Defining Ethical Criteria:

Ethical investors establish criteria for their investment choices. We explore the art of defining ethical guidelines that guide the investment process.

3. The Influence of Environmental Impact:

Ethical investing emphasizes environmental considerations. We discuss the art of investing in companies with sustainable practices and low carbon footprints.

4. The Power of Social Responsibility:

Ethical investing addresses social issues and promotes social responsibility. We explore the art of supporting companies that prioritize fair labor practices and diversity.

    5. The Art of Corporate Governance Assessment:

Ethical investors focus on companies with strong governance practices. We discuss the art of evaluating board diversity, executive compensation, and shareholder rights.

    6. The Influence of United Nations Sustainable Development Goals (SDGs):

Ethical investing aligns with the United Nations SDGs. We explore the art of targeting investments that contribute to achieving these global goals.

    7. The Art of Positive Screening:

Positive screening involves selecting companies based on ethical criteria. We discuss the art of identifying companies that align with investors' values.

    8. The Power of Negative Screening:

Negative screening excludes companies with certain activities or practices. We explore the art of avoiding investments in industries like tobacco, weapons, or fossil fuels.

    9. The Art of Thematic Investing:

Thematic investing focuses on specific social or environmental themes. We discuss the art of targeting investments in areas like renewable energy or healthcare innovation.

    10. The Influence of Impact Investing:

Impact investing seeks measurable positive outcomes. We explore the art of investing in projects that drive social and environmental change.

    11. The Art of Community Investing:

Community investing supports underserved communities. We discuss the art of financing projects that promote economic development and social inclusion.

    12. The Power of Engaging with Companies:

Ethical investors engage with companies to drive positive change. We explore the art of shareholder advocacy and proxy voting to influence corporate behavior.

13. The Art of Integrating ESG Factors:

ESG factors assess a company's environmental, social, and governance practices. We discuss the art of incorporating ESG analysis into investment decisions.

14. The Influence of Ethical Exchange-Traded Funds (ETFs):

Ethical ETFs offer diversified exposure to socially responsible investments. We explore the art of selecting ethical ETFs aligned with investors' values.

15. The Art of Green Bonds:

Green bonds fund environmentally friendly projects. We discuss the art of investing in green bonds to support sustainability initiatives.

16. The Power of Ethical Mutual Funds:

Ethical mutual funds invest in accordance with ethical principles. We explore the art of selecting mutual funds that align with investors' values.

17. The Art of Measuring Impact:

Ethical investors seek to measure their impact on society and the environment. We discuss the art of assessing the tangible outcomes of ethical investments.

18. The Influence of Ethical Robo-Advisors:

Ethical robo-advisors offer automated ethical investment solutions. We explore the art of using robo-advisors to build diversified ethical portfolios.

19. The Art of Supporting Clean Technology:

Clean technology addresses environmental challenges. We discuss the art of investing in companies driving innovation in clean energy and sustainability.

20. The Power of Sustainable Agriculture:

Ethical investing supports sustainable agriculture practices. We explore the art of investing in companies promoting responsible farming methods.

21. The Art of Philanthropy and Impact Philanthropy:

Ethical investors may engage in impact philanthropy. We discuss the art of aligning charitable giving with ethical investment goals.

22. The Influence of Ethical Real Estate Investing:

Ethical real estate investing prioritizes sustainability and community development. We explore the art of investing in properties with positive social impact.

23. The Art of Avoiding Controversial Industries:

Ethical investors avoid controversial industries with negative societal impacts. We discuss the art of divesting from businesses that conflict with ethical values.

24. The Power of Ethical Leadership Assessment:

Ethical leaders drive corporate responsibility. We explore the art of assessing leadership commitment to ethical practices.

25. The Art of Investing in Social Enterprises:

Social enterprises blend profit with purpose. We discuss the art of supporting businesses that tackle social challenges.

26. The Influence of Ethical Microfinance:

Ethical microfinance supports financial inclusion in underserved communities. We explore the art of investing in microfinance projects.

27. The Art of Ethical Investor Education:

Ethical investors prioritize financial literacy and ethical education. We discuss the art of educating oneself and others about the principles of ethical investing.

28. The Power of Ethical Supply Chain Analysis:

Ethical investing considers companies' supply chain practices. We explore the art of evaluating ethical supply chain management.

29. The Art of Assessing Ethical Leadership:

Ethical leaders drive positive change within companies. We discuss the art of identifying companies with ethical leadership.

30. The Influence of Ethical Bond Investing:

Ethical bonds fund projects with positive social or environmental impact. We explore the art of investing in green, social, and sustainable bonds.

31. The Art of Corporate Impact Reporting:

Ethical investors value transparent impact reporting. We discuss the art of holding companies accountable for their ethical commitments.

32. The Power of Ethical Venture Capital:

Ethical venture capital supports socially conscious startups. We explore the art of investing in companies that address societal challenges.

33. The Art of Promoting Diversity and Inclusion:

Ethical investors value diversity and inclusion in corporate settings. We discuss the art of supporting companies with inclusive practices.

34. The Influence of Ethical Risk Management:

Ethical risk management considers broader societal implications. We explore the art of integrating ethical risk assessment into investment strategies.

35. The Art of Ethical Currency Investing:

Ethical currency investing considers macroeconomic impacts.

We discuss the art of managing currency exposure in alignment with ethical principles.

36. The Power of Ethical Hedge Funds:

Ethical hedge funds apply responsible investment strategies. We explore the art of selecting hedge funds with ethical principles.

37. The Art of Climate Change Investing:

Ethical investors address climate change challenges. We discuss the art of investing in companies promoting climate resilience.

38. The Influence of Ethical Artificial Intelligence:

Ethical AI investing considers the social implications of AI technology. We explore the art of investing in companies with responsible AI practices.

Conclusion:

"The Art of Ethical Investing" celebrates the transformative potential of aligning investments with personal values and societal goals. Just as an artist uses their talents to create meaningful and impactful works of art, ethical investors use their financial resources to create positive change in the world. By embracing the art of ethical investing, individuals and institutions can contribute to a more sustainable and inclusive future, while achieving their financial objectives.

CHAPTER 40: THE ARTFUL NEGOTIATOR: ENHANCING YOUR INVESTMENT SKILLS

Introduction:

In Chapter 40, "The Artful Negotiator: Enhancing Your Investment Skills," we explore the critical role of negotiation in the world of investing. Negotiation is the art of arriving at mutually beneficial agreements, and it plays a pivotal role in various investment activities, from deal-making to managing portfolio positions. This chapter delves into the principles of effective negotiation, the key skills required, and how mastering the art of negotiation can lead to more profitable investment outcomes.

1. The Significance of Negotiation in Investing:

Negotiation is pervasive in investing, from striking deals with asset sellers to negotiating contract terms. We discuss the importance of negotiation skills in enhancing investment success.

2. The Art of Building Rapport:

Effective negotiation begins with building rapport. We explore the art of establishing trust and a positive relationship with counterparties.

3. The Influence of Emotional Intelligence:

Emotional intelligence is essential for successful negotiation. We discuss the art of understanding and managing emotions in investment negotiations.

4. The Power of Active Listening:

Active listening is a cornerstone of effective negotiation.

We explore the art of fully understanding the needs and perspectives of other parties.

5. The Art of Preparation:

Preparation is crucial in investment negotiations. We discuss the art of conducting thorough research and analysis before entering negotiations.

6. The Influence of BATNA (Best Alternative to a Negotiated Agreement):

BATNA guides negotiation strategy. We explore the art of identifying and leveraging BATNA to achieve favorable outcomes.

7. The Art of Setting Objectives:

Clear objectives drive successful negotiations. We discuss the art of defining specific and measurable goals for investment negotiations.

8. The Power of Negotiation Leverage:

Leverage affects negotiation dynamics. We explore the art of assessing and leveraging negotiation power in investment transactions.

9. The Art of Win-Win Negotiation:

Win-win negotiation fosters long-term relationships. We discuss the art of creating mutually beneficial outcomes for all parties involved.

10. The Influence of Cultural Awareness:

Negotiating across cultures requires sensitivity. We explore the art of navigating cultural differences in international investment dealings.

11. The Art of Negotiating Investment Terms:

Investment terms determine deal profitability. We discuss the art of securing favorable terms in investment agreements.

12. The Power of Negotiating with Venture Capitalists:

Startups negotiate with venture capitalists for funding. We explore the art of presenting compelling investment cases to attract VC investments.

13. The Art of Negotiating with Investment Partners:

Investment partnerships require negotiation. We discuss the art of structuring equitable terms and responsibilities with co-investors.

14. The Influence of Negotiating with Portfolio Companies:

Investors negotiate with portfolio companies for growth and performance. We explore the art of collaborating with management teams for success.

15. The Art of Valuation Negotiation:

Valuation negotiations are critical in investment deals. We discuss the art of arriving at fair valuations based on data and analysis.

16. The Power of Negotiating with Investment Advisors:

Investors negotiate with advisors for strategic guidance. We explore the art of selecting advisors and setting clear expectations.

17. The Art of Managing Disagreements:

Disagreements are common in negotiations. We discuss the art of handling conflicts and finding common ground.

18. The Influence of Negotiating Exit Strategies:

Exit negotiations determine investment returns. We explore the art of planning and executing exit strategies with multiple stakeholders.

19. The Art of Negotiating with Debt Providers:

Debt financing involves negotiation. We discuss the art of securing favorable debt terms and covenants.

20. The Power of Negotiating Joint Ventures:

Joint ventures require intricate negotiations. We explore the art of structuring joint ventures for mutual benefits.

21. The Art of Negotiating in Distressed Situations:

Distressed investments involve complex negotiations. We discuss the art of managing negotiations in challenging market conditions.

22. The Influence of Negotiating with Regulators:

Negotiating with regulators impacts investment compliance. We explore the art of engaging constructively with regulatory authorities.

23. The Art of Negotiating in Public-Private Partnerships:

Public-private partnerships require negotiation with government entities. We discuss the art of balancing public interests with private sector goals.

24. The Power of Negotiating Mergers and Acquisitions:

M&A negotiations are critical for deal success. We explore the art of navigating complex negotiations in mergers and acquisitions.

25. The Art of Negotiating in Real Estate Investment:

Real estate negotiations involve multiple parties. We discuss the art of reaching agreements in real estate transactions.

26. The Influence of Negotiating with Investment Bankers:

Investment bankers facilitate deals and require negotiation. We explore the art of engaging with bankers for investment opportunities.

27. The Art of Negotiating Investment Terms in Private Equity:

Private equity deals involve intricate negotiations. We discuss the art of structuring private equity investments for optimal returns.

28. The Power of Negotiating in Public Offerings:

Public offerings involve negotiations with underwriters and regulators. We explore the art of preparing and executing successful public offerings.

29. The Art of Negotiating with Angel Investors:

Startups negotiate with angel investors for seed funding. We discuss the art of presenting compelling investment cases to attract angel investments.

30. The Influence of Negotiating with Institutional Investors:

Institutional investors negotiate large-scale investments. We explore the art of dealing with institutional investors and their specific requirements.

31. The Art of Negotiating in Global Investments:

Global investments involve diverse negotiation styles. We discuss the art of adapting negotiation techniques for cross-border deals.

32. The Power of Negotiating with Shareholders:

Investors negotiate with shareholders for corporate actions. We explore the art of managing shareholder expectations and voting rights.

33. The Art of Negotiating with Family Offices:

Family offices require personalized negotiations. We discuss the art of engaging with family offices for investment opportunities.

34. The Influence of Negotiating in Hedge Fund Investments:

Hedge fund investments involve unique terms. We explore the art of negotiating with hedge funds to meet specific investment objectives.

35. The Art of Negotiating in Private Placements:

Private placements require negotiation with issuers. We discuss the art of participating in private placement offerings.

36. The Power of Negotiating with Suppliers and Partners:

Negotiating with suppliers affects investment costs. We explore the art of securing favorable terms with business partners.

37. The Art of Negotiating in Infrastructure Investment:

Infrastructure deals involve negotiation with government entities. We discuss the art of structuring infrastructure investments with long-term benefits.

38. The Influence of Negotiating with Industry Regulators:

Negotiating with regulators affects investment compliance. We explore the art of engaging constructively with industry regulators.

39. The Art of Negotiating in Technology Investments:

Technology investments involve intellectual property negotiations. We discuss the art of securing IP rights and licensing agreements.

40. The Power of Negotiating in Impact Investing:

Impact investing requires negotiating for social outcomes. We explore the art of measuring impact and aligning with investee goals.

Conclusion:

"The Artful Negotiator: Enhancing Your Investment Skills" celebrates the transformative impact of negotiation in the world of investing. Just as an artist hones their craft through practice and refinement, investors gain mastery in negotiation by developing and refining their negotiation skills. By embracing the art of negotiation, investors can unlock new opportunities, maximize investment returns, and build strong relationships within the financial ecosystem.

In the tapestry of investment success, the art of negotiation becomes a brushstroke that adds finesse, resilience, and strategic acumen to the canvas of financial prosperity. As investors navigate the complexities of the financial landscape, the art of negotiation becomes an indispensable skill that empowers them to make well-informed decisions, structure favorable deals, and create sustainable investment partnerships. Through this profound understanding and application of negotiation principles, investors can confidently and artfully paint their financial futures with colors of opportunity, collaboration, and mutual benefit.

Ultimately, the artful negotiator is not just focused on securing the best possible deal for themselves but seeks to create win-win situations that benefit all parties involved. By mastering the art of negotiation, investors can contribute to a more harmonious and interconnected financial ecosystem, where collaboration, trust, and shared goals lead to prosperity and progress.

As investors continue to evolve in their roles as artful negotiators, they must remember that negotiation is not solely about tactics and strategies; it is also about fostering meaningful connections, understanding diverse perspectives, and finding common ground. The artful negotiator approaches every negotiation as an opportunity for growth, learning, and building lasting relationships. By integrating these principles into their investment approach, investors can elevate their negotiation skills to an art form, leaving a lasting positive impact on their investment journey and the financial landscape as a whole.

In conclusion, "The Artful Negotiator: Enhancing Your Investment Skills" serves as a guide for investors to sharpen their negotiation prowess, drawing on the expertise of master negotiators and the timeless principles of effective negotiation. Just as an artist paints with precision and passion, the artful negotiator crafts investment deals with finesse and strategic foresight. By embracing the art of negotiation, investors can navigate the dynamic and ever-changing world of investing with confidence, competence, and conviction, creating a masterpiece of financial success and meaningful impact on their journey towards prosperity.

CHAPTER 41: THE ART OF STOCK PICKING

Introduction:

In Chapter 41, "The Art of Stock Picking," we delve into the art and science of selecting individual stocks for investment portfolios. Stock picking is a fundamental aspect of equity investing, where investors seek to identify companies with strong growth prospects, sound fundamentals, and attractive valuations. This chapter explores the various methodologies and strategies employed by successful stock pickers, the role of research and analysis, and the key factors to consider when selecting stocks to build a diversified and profitable portfolio.

1. The Significance of Stock Picking:

Stock picking is at the heart of active equity investing. We discuss the importance of selecting the right stocks to achieve superior investment returns.

2. The Art of Identifying Growth Stocks:

Growth stocks offer the potential for above-average earnings growth. We explore the art of identifying companies poised for rapid expansion.

3. The Influence of Value Investing:

Value investing focuses on undervalued stocks. We discuss the art of finding companies with attractive valuations relative to their intrinsic worth.

4. The Power of Dividend Investing:

Dividend investing emphasizes companies with consistent dividends. We explore the art of selecting dividend-paying stocks for income and growth.

5. The Art of Evaluating Company Fundamentals:

Company fundamentals drive stock performance. We discuss the art of analyzing financial statements, revenue growth, profit margins, and debt levels.

6. The Influence of Industry and Sector Analysis:

Industry and sector dynamics impact stock performance. We explore the art of analyzing macroeconomic trends and competitive landscapes.

7. The Art of Conducting Technical Analysis:

Technical analysis assesses historical stock price patterns. We discuss the art of using charts and indicators to make buy and sell decisions.

8. The Power of Management Assessment:

Strong management is essential for company success. We explore the art of evaluating leadership capabilities and corporate governance.

9. The Art of Gauging Competitive Advantages:

Competitive advantages drive long-term profitability. We discuss the art of identifying companies with sustainable moats.

10. The Influence of Market Capitalization:

Market capitalization impacts investment risk and potential returns. We explore the art of selecting stocks across small-cap, mid-cap, and large-cap categories.

11. The Art of Assessing Growth Prospects:

Growth prospects determine stock potential. We discuss the art of forecasting revenue and earnings growth for companies.

12. The Power of Analyzing Price-to-Earnings Ratio (P/E):

P/E ratio assesses stock valuations. We explore the art of using P/E ratios to identify attractively priced stocks.

13. The Art of Recognizing Market Trends:

Market trends influence stock performance. We discuss the art of identifying and capitalizing on market trends.

14. The Influence of Risk Management:

Risk management is crucial in stock picking. We explore the art of balancing risk and reward in investment decisions.

15. The Art of Monitoring Market Sentiment:

Market sentiment impacts stock prices. We discuss the art of interpreting investor sentiment and its effects on stock movements.

16. The Power of Company Research and Due Diligence:

Thorough research drives informed stock picking. We explore the art of conducting comprehensive due diligence on potential investments.

17. The Art of Managing a Watchlist:

A watchlist helps track potential stock candidates. We discuss the art of organizing and maintaining a watchlist for timely stock picks.

18. The Influence of Global Economic Analysis:

Global economic trends impact stock markets. We explore the art of incorporating macroeconomic analysis into stock selection.

19. The Art of Long-Term Investing:

Long-term investing emphasizes patience and discipline. We discuss the art of identifying stocks with enduring growth prospects.

20. The Power of Fundamental vs. Technical Analysis:

Fundamental and technical analysis offer different perspectives. We explore the art of combining both approaches for robust stock picking.

21. The Art of Contrarian Investing:

Contrarian investing involves going against market trends. We discuss the art of identifying opportunities when market sentiment is overly pessimistic.

22. The Influence of Environmental, Social, and Governance (ESG) Factors:

ESG considerations influence stock performance. We explore the art of integrating ESG analysis into stock selection.

23. The Art of Investing in Emerging Markets:

Emerging markets offer growth opportunities. We discuss the art of evaluating companies in developing economies.

24. The Power of Behavioral Finance:

Behavioral finance impacts investor decisions. We explore the art of recognizing behavioral biases in stock picking.

25. The Art of Sector Rotation:

Sector rotation involves shifting investments across industries. We discuss the art of capitalizing on sector-specific trends.

26. The Influence of Technical Indicators:

Technical indicators guide stock entry and exit points. We explore the art of using moving averages, RSI, and other indicators in stock picking.

27. The Art of Evaluating Financial Health:

Financial health indicates company stability. We discuss the art of assessing debt-to-equity ratios, cash flow, and liquidity.

28. The Power of Growth vs. Value Bias:

Growth and value stocks offer different risk-reward profiles. We explore the art of balancing growth and value bias in stock selection.

29. The Art of Selecting Dividend Growth Stocks:

Dividend growth stocks combine income and appreciation.

We discuss the art of identifying companies with sustainable dividend growth.

30. The Influence of Market Capitalization Bias:

Market capitalization bias impacts portfolio risk. We explore the art of maintaining a diversified mix of small, mid, and large-cap stocks.

31. The Art of Portfolio Monitoring and Rebalancing:

Stock portfolios require regular review and rebalancing. We discuss the art of adjusting allocations based on changing market conditions.

32. The Power of Stock Screening Tools:

Stock screening tools facilitate stock selection. We explore the art of using screeners to identify promising stocks.

33. The Art of Understanding Economic Indicators:

Economic indicators influence stock performance. We discuss the art of interpreting GDP, inflation, and unemployment data.

34. The Influence of Sector ETFs:

Sector ETFs offer exposure to specific industries. We explore the art of using sector ETFs for targeted stock picking.

35. The Art of Investing in High-Quality Stocks:

High-quality stocks offer stability and growth potential. We discuss the art of investing in companies with strong fundamentals.

36. The Power of Investing in Innovators:

Innovative companies drive disruptive growth. We explore the art of identifying firms at the forefront of innovation.

37. The Art of Assessing Competitive Landscape:

Competitive analysis helps identify market leaders. We discuss the art of evaluating companies' positioning in their industries.

38. The Influence of Stock Diversification:

Diversification reduces portfolio risk. We explore the art of diversifying across industries and geographies.

39. The Art of Investing in IPOs:

IPOs offer opportunities and risks. We discuss the art of evaluating newly listed companies.

40. The Power of Patience and Discipline:

Patience and discipline are essential in stock picking. We explore the art of sticking to investment strategies amid market fluctuations.

Conclusion:

"The Art of Stock Picking" celebrates the intricate and dynamic process of selecting individual stocks that drive investment returns and portfolio growth. Just as an artist carefully chooses colors and brushstrokes to craft a masterpiece, stock pickers meticulously analyze data, market trends, and company fundamentals to construct well-constructed investment portfolios. By embracing the art of stock picking, investors can enhance their ability to identify promising investment opportunities, navigate through market uncertainties, and achieve their financial objectives.

As investors continue to refine their skills in the art of stock picking, they must remember that successful stock selection goes beyond simple guesswork or short-term speculation.

CHAPTER 42: THE POWER OF ARTFUL NETWORKING IN INVESTING

Introduction:

In Chapter 42, "The Power of Artful Networking in Investing," we explore the profound impact of networking on investment success. Networking is the art of building and nurturing professional relationships with individuals in the financial industry and beyond. For investors, artful networking plays a crucial role in sourcing investment opportunities, gaining valuable insights, and accessing a broader pool of resources and expertise. This chapter delves into the principles of effective networking, strategies for expanding one's network, and the transformative benefits of fostering meaningful connections in the world of investing.

1. The Significance of Networking in Investing:

Networking is a cornerstone of successful investing. We discuss the importance of cultivating a robust network to access unique investment opportunities and expertise.

2. The Art of Building Meaningful Relationships:

Meaningful relationships drive fruitful networking. We explore the art of nurturing authentic connections with industry peers, professionals, and experts.

3. The Influence of Industry Conferences and Events:

Industry conferences offer networking opportunities. We discuss the art of engaging with like-minded investors and thought leaders at events.

4. The Power of Online Networking:

Online platforms facilitate global networking. We explore the art of leveraging social media, investment forums, and virtual events to expand one's network.

5. The Art of Elevator Pitching:

An elevator pitch showcases investment goals. We discuss the art of succinctly presenting oneself and investment objectives to potential partners.

6. The Influence of Mentorship and Coaching:

Mentors offer guidance and support in investing. We explore the art of seeking mentorship and learning from experienced investors.

7. The Power of Investment Clubs and Groups:

Investment clubs promote collaborative learning. We discuss the art of participating in clubs to share investment ideas and research.

8. The Art of Attending Investor Meetups:

Investor meetups foster local networking. We explore the art of engaging with investors in one's community.

9. The Influence of Alumni Networks:

Alumni networks provide valuable connections. We discuss the art of leveraging educational and professional alumni associations.

10. The Power of Referrals and Introductions:

Referrals expand one's network. We explore the art of requesting and providing introductions to potential investment partners.

11. The Art of Active Listening:

Active listening enhances networking effectiveness. We discuss the art of attentively understanding others' perspectives and investment insights.

12. The Influence of Building a Personal Brand:

A strong personal brand attracts opportunities. We explore the art of showcasing expertise and credibility to attract like-minded investors.

13. The Power of Networking in Deal Sourcing:

Networking facilitates deal flow. We discuss the art of sourcing investment opportunities through connections.

14. The Art of Cultivating Industry Relationships:

Industry relationships foster collaboration. We explore the art of forging partnerships with key players in the financial sector.

15. The Influence of Networking in Due Diligence:

Networking aids in thorough due diligence. We discuss the art of accessing information and expertise to make informed investment decisions.

16. The Power of Cross-Industry Networking:

Cross-industry networking sparks innovation. We explore the art of learning from diverse industries to identify new investment trends.

17. The Art of Networking with Entrepreneurs:

Entrepreneurs offer unique investment opportunities. We discuss the art of connecting with founders and startups for potential investments.

18. The Influence of Networking with Institutional Investors:

Institutional investors provide valuable insights. We explore the art of engaging with institutions for market intelligence.

19. The Power of Networking in Emerging Markets:

Networking opens doors in emerging markets. We discuss the art of developing relationships in regions with high growth potential.

20. The Art of Engaging with Investment Advisors:

Investment advisors offer valuable perspectives. We explore the art of collaborating with experts for tailored investment strategies.

21. The Influence of Networking in Real Estate Investing:

Networking aids in real estate deal sourcing. We discuss the art of connecting with brokers, developers, and property owners.

22. The Power of Networking in Private Equity:

Private equity connections drive deal flow. We explore the art of accessing exclusive investment opportunities through networking.

23. The Art of Networking in Venture Capital:

Venture capitalists rely on extensive networks. We discuss the art of building connections with entrepreneurs and startup ecosystems.

24. The Influence of Networking in Hedge Funds:

Networking benefits hedge fund investors. We explore the art of accessing unique hedge fund strategies through connections.

25. The Power of Networking with Family Offices:

Family offices provide diverse investment opportunities. We discuss the art of connecting with family offices for co-investments.

26. The Art of Networking for International Investments:

Networking opens doors in global markets. We explore the art of establishing connections for international investment opportunities.

27. The Influence of Networking in Impact Investing:

Networking supports impact investing goals. We discuss the art of collaborating with impact-driven investors and organizations.

28. The Power of Networking with Industry Regulators:

Regulatory connections offer insights. We explore the art of engaging constructively with regulatory authorities.

29. The Art of Networking for Market Insights:

Networking facilitates market intelligence. We discuss the art of accessing valuable market trends and analysis through connections.

30. The Influence of Networking in Fundraising:

Networking aids in fundraising efforts. We explore the art of connecting with potential investors for raising capital.

31. The Power of Networking for Co-Investment Opportunities:

Co-investing leverages collective expertise. We discuss the art of forming co-investment partnerships through networking.

32. The Art of Networking with Startups:

Startups seek investors through networking. We explore the art of identifying promising startups through connections.

33. The Influence of Networking in ESG Investing:

Networking supports ESG integration. We discuss the art of engaging with ESG experts and sustainable finance practitioners.

34. The Power of Networking with Industry Analysts:

Industry analysts provide market insights. We explore the art of connecting with analysts for investment research.

35. The Art of Networking for Angel Investments:

Angel investors collaborate through networks. We discuss the art of participating in angel investor communities.

36. The Influence of Networking in Alternative Investments:

Networking aids in alternative asset access. We explore the art of connecting with providers of unique investment opportunities.

37. The Power of Networking for Due Diligence:

Networking supports comprehensive due diligence. We discuss the art of accessing expert opinions and insights for decision-making.

38. The Art of Networking for Philanthropic Investing:

Networking aids in philanthropic investments. We explore the art of connecting with impact-focused foundations and organizations.

39. The Influence of Networking in Pre-IPO Investing:

Networking provides access to pre-IPO opportunities. We discuss the art of accessing shares in companies before going public.

40. The Power of Networking for Secondary Market Investments:

Secondary markets offer networking opportunities. We explore the art of connecting with sellers and buyers of pre-owned investments.

Conclusion:

"The Power of Artful Networking in Investing" celebrates the transformative potential of building and nurturing professional relationships in the world of finance. Just as an artist blends colors and textures to create a masterpiece, investors skillfully cultivate their networks to access unique investment opportunities, gain valuable insights, and broaden their horizons. By embracing the art of networking, investors can expand their reach, navigate through complex investment landscapes, and create a powerful network of like-minded individuals and industry experts.

In the canvas of investment success, artful networking becomes a brushstroke that adds depth, connectivity, and opportunity to the portfolio of an astute investor.

CHAPTER 43: PAINTING A LEGACY: INVESTING FOR FUTURE GENERATIONS

Introduction:

In Chapter 43, "Painting a Legacy: Investing for Future Generations," we explore the profound impact of long-term investing and wealth preservation with a focus on creating a lasting legacy for future generations. Investing for the future is not only about generating financial returns; it's about leaving behind a meaningful and sustainable legacy that benefits one's family, community, and society at large. This chapter delves into the principles of generational investing, strategies for wealth preservation, and the transformative benefits of building a legacy that transcends time.

1. The Significance of Generational Investing:

Generational investing emphasizes long-term vision. We discuss the importance of preserving wealth and creating a financial legacy for future generations.

2. The Art of Building a Multigenerational Investment Plan:

A multigenerational plan aligns family goals. We explore the art of creating investment strategies that span across generations.

3. The Influence of Legacy Planning:

Legacy planning guides investment decisions. We discuss the art of integrating family values and philanthropy into investment goals.

4. The Power of Compounding: The Timeless Magic of Patience:

Compounding creates enduring wealth. We explore the art of harnessing the power of patience in investment decisions.

5. The Art of Diversifying Across Asset Classes:

Diversification mitigates risk across generations. We discuss the art of constructing resilient portfolios with a mix of assets.

6. The Influence of Intergenerational Communication:

Communication fosters family cohesion. We explore the art of engaging with family members to align on investment values and goals.

7. The Power of Philanthropic Investing:

Philanthropy leaves a lasting impact. We discuss the art of integrating charitable giving and social impact in investment strategies.

8. The Art of Sustainable and ESG Investing:

Sustainable investing promotes responsible practices. We explore the art of aligning investments with environmental, social, and governance principles.

9. The Influence of Education and Financial Literacy:

Financial literacy empowers future generations. We discuss the art of educating heirs about investment principles and responsible stewardship.

10. The Power of Trusts and Estate Planning:

Trusts safeguard wealth for heirs. We explore the art of structuring estate plans to preserve assets across generations.

11. The Art of Investing in Education and Human Capital:

Investing in human capital benefits society. We discuss the art of supporting education and skill development for future generations.

12. The Influence of Tax-Efficient Strategies:

Tax efficiency enhances wealth preservation. We explore the art of minimizing tax burdens across generations.

13. The Power of Long-Term Vision in Business Investing:

Investing in businesses creates enduring value. We discuss the art of supporting businesses with lasting potential.

14. The Art of Family Governance:

Family governance promotes unity. We explore the art of establishing governance structures to sustain investment legacies.

15. The Influence of Responsible Stewardship:

Stewardship safeguards family assets. We discuss the art of instilling responsible practices in managing wealth.

16. The Power of Adaptive Investing:

Adaptive investing responds to changing times. We explore the art of adjusting investment strategies to meet evolving family needs.

17. The Art of Balancing Current and Future Needs:

Balancing present and future goals are key. We discuss the art of making investment decisions that benefit current and future generations.

18. The Influence of Socially Responsible Investing:

Socially responsible investing aligns with family values. We explore the art of incorporating ethical considerations into investment choices.

19. The Power of Generational Collaboration:

Generational collaboration fosters continuity. We discuss the art of involving multiple generations in investment decisions.

20. The Art of Investing in Innovation and Technology:

Investing in innovation drives progress. We explore the art of supporting technologies that shape the future.

21. The Influence of Global Investing:

Global investing transcends borders. We discuss the art of diversifying investments across international markets.

22. The Power of Community Impact Investing:

Community impact investing empowers local change. We explore the art of supporting projects that benefit the community.

23. The Art of Charitable Foundations and Endowments:

Charitable foundations leave a lasting legacy. We discuss the art of establishing foundations and endowments for social causes.

24. The Influence of Family Philanthropy:

Family philanthropy builds unity. We explore the art of engaging family members in philanthropic efforts.

25. The Power of Long-Term Real Estate Investments:

Real estate investments appreciate over time. We discuss the art of preserving wealth through property ownership.

26. The Art of Navigating Generational Wealth Transfers:

Wealth transfers require careful planning. We explore the art of transferring assets smoothly to future generations.

27. The Influence of Cultural Heritage Investing:

Cultural heritage investing preserves traditions. We discuss the art of investing in projects that honor cultural heritage.

28. The Power of Environmental Conservation Investing:

Environmental conservation investing protects the planet. We explore the art of supporting sustainable initiatives.

29. The Art of Impactful Mentorship:

Mentorship shapes future leaders. We discuss the art of mentoring heirs to carry on investment legacies.

30. The Influence of Building Financial Resilience:

Financial resilience prepares for uncertainties. We explore the art of building robust financial plans for future generations.

31. The Power of Estate Protection Strategies:

Estate protection safeguards wealth. We discuss the art of minimizing risks to family assets.

32. The Art of Preserving Intellectual Property:

Intellectual property drives innovation. We explore the art of protecting family inventions and creations.

33. The Influence of Family Values in Investing:

Family values guide investment decisions. We discuss the art of aligning investments with ethical principles.

34. The Power of Ethical Leadership in Business:

Ethical business leadership sets an example. We explore the art of supporting businesses with strong moral compasses.

35. The Art of Managing Intergenerational Expectations:

Managing expectations fosters harmony. We discuss the art of addressing differing perspectives on investment strategies.

36. The Influence of Responsible Governance:

Responsible governance ensures sustainability. We explore the art of upholding ethical practices in family businesses.

37. The Power of Social Entrepreneurship:

Social entrepreneurship addresses societal challenges. We discuss the art of investing in businesses with positive social impact.

38. The Art of Cultivating Family Traditions:

Family traditions strengthen bonds. We explore the art of incorporating investment discussions into family rituals.

39. The Influence of Adaptive Philanthropy:

Adaptive philanthropy addresses changing needs. We discuss the art of flexibly responding to emerging social issues.

40. The Power of Empowering Future Generations:

Empowering future generations secures the legacy. We explore the art of nurturing confident and responsible heirs.

Conclusion:

"Painting a Legacy: Investing for Future Generations" celebrates the transformative potential of investing with a multigenerational vision and a commitment to leaving behind a lasting legacy. Just as an artist creates a masterpiece with meticulous care and attention, investors carefully craft their financial legacies to benefit their families, communities, and society at large for generations to come.

CHAPTER 44: THE ART OF ENTREPRENEURIAL INVESTING

Introduction:

In Chapter 44, "The Art of Entrepreneurial Investing," we explore the dynamic world of venture capital and angel investing, where investors play a crucial role in supporting and fueling the growth of early-stage companies and startups. Entrepreneurial investing goes beyond traditional asset classes, offering the opportunity to invest in innovative ventures that have the potential for exponential growth. This chapter delves into the principles of entrepreneurial investing, strategies for identifying promising startups, and the transformative benefits of supporting the next generation of disruptive businesses.

1. The Significance of Entrepreneurial Investing:

Entrepreneurial investing drives innovation and economic growth. We discuss the importance of backing early-stage companies with high growth potential.

2. The Art of Assessing Market Disruptions:

Market disruptions offer investment opportunities. We explore the art of identifying startups that challenge existing industries.

3. The Influence of Angel Investing:

Angel investors provide vital seed capital. We discuss the art of supporting startups in their initial stages.

4. The Power of Venture Capital:

Venture capital funds fuel growth. We explore the art of investing in startups with established track records and growth potential.

5. The Art of Evaluating Entrepreneurial Teams:

The founding team is key to startup success. We discuss the art of assessing the expertise and passion of entrepreneurs.

6. The Influence of Market Traction and Proof of Concept:

Market traction validates startup viability. We explore the art of gauging early success and potential scalability.

7. The Power of Sector and Industry Analysis:

Sector analysis guides entrepreneurial investments. We discuss the art of focusing on specific industries with high growth potential.

8. The Art of Conducting Due Diligence on Startups:

Due diligence minimizes investment risks. We explore the art of assessing startup financials, market fit, and competitive advantage.

9. The Influence of Startup Valuations:

Startup valuations impact investment decisions. We discuss the art of determining fair valuations for early-stage companies.

10. The Power of Portfolio Diversification:

Diversification reduces startup investment risks. We explore the art of spreading investments across multiple ventures.

11. The Art of Investing in Disruptive Technologies:

Disruptive technologies transform industries. We discuss the art of backing startups with innovative solutions.

12. The Influence of the Lean Startup Model:

The lean startup approach fosters efficiency. We explore the art of supporting startups with lean and agile methodologies.

13. The Power of Mentorship and Value-Add Investing:

Mentors enhance startup success. We discuss the art of providing expertise and guidance to portfolio companies.

14. The Art of Supporting Female and Minority Entrepreneurs:

Diversity drives innovation. We explore the art of promoting inclusion and backing underrepresented founders.

15. The Influence of Seed Funding and Pre-Seed Investments:

Seed funding kickstarts startup growth. We discuss the art of investing in early rounds to support initial progress.

16. The Power of Growth Stage Investing:

Growth stage investments fuel expansion. We explore the art of backing startups that have demonstrated market potential.

17. The Art of Investing in Emerging Markets:

Emerging markets offer untapped potential. We discuss the art of identifying startups in growing economies.

18. The Influence of Startup Ecosystems:

Thriving ecosystems nurture startups. We explore the art of investing in regions with robust startup support.

19. The Power of Collaborative Investing:

Collaborative investing pools resources. We discuss the art of co-investing with other angel investors and venture capitalists.

20. The Art of Understanding Regulatory Environment:

Regulations impact startup operations. We explore the art of assessing the regulatory landscape for startups.

21. The Influence of Intellectual Property Evaluation:

Intellectual property safeguards startup assets. We discuss the art of assessing a startup's IP portfolio.

22. The Power of Timing in Entrepreneurial Investing:

Timing affects startup success. We explore the art of investing at opportune moments in a startup's growth trajectory.

23. The Art of Exit Strategies:

Exit strategies provide liquidity. We discuss the art of planning for successful exits through acquisitions or IPOs.

24. The Influence of Crowdfunding and Online Platforms:

Online platforms democratize startup investing. We explore the art of leveraging crowdfunding and investment portals.

25. The Power of Measuring Startup Impact:

Startup impact goes beyond financial returns. We discuss the art of evaluating social, environmental, and technological impacts.

26. The Art of Managing Risk in Entrepreneurial Investing:

Risk management is vital in startup investing. We explore the art of balancing risk and reward in venture capital.

27. The Influence of Networking in Startup Investing:

Networking expands deal flow. We discuss the art of accessing startup opportunities through connections.

28. The Power of Corporate Venture Capital:

Corporate venture capital drives innovation. We explore the art of corporations investing in startups.

29. The Art of Investing in AI and Tech Startups:

AI and tech startups disrupt industries. We discuss the art of supporting ventures at the forefront of technological advancements.

30. The Influence of Accelerators and Incubators:

Accelerators and incubators nurture startups. We explore the art of investing in companies that have benefited from these programs.

31. The Power of Founder-Friendly Terms:

Founder-friendly terms foster positive relationships. We discuss the art of providing fair and supportive deal structures.

32. The Art of Identifying Scalable Business Models:

Scalability drives startup success. We explore the art of

assessing business models with growth potential.

33. The Influence of Startup Branding and Marketing:

Strong branding attracts customers and investors. We discuss the art of supporting startups with effective marketing strategies.

34. The Power of Investing in Clean Energy Startups:

Clean energy solutions address environmental challenges. We explore the art of backing startups focused on sustainability.

35. The Art of Adapting to Market Changes:

Adaptability is key in startup investing. We discuss the art of responding to market shifts and evolving business strategies.

36. The Influence of Early Adopter Analysis:

Early adopters validate startups' value propositions. We explore the art of identifying startups with enthusiastic user bases.

37. The Power of Supporting HealthTech and MedTech Ventures:

HealthTech and MedTech improve healthcare outcomes. We discuss the art of investing in startups driving medical advancements.

38. The Art of Supporting Social Enterprises:

Social enterprises create positive change. We explore the art of investing in ventures with social impact missions.

39. The Influence of Impact Measurement:

Measuring impact informs investment decisions. We discuss the art of assessing startups' progress toward social and environmental goals.

40. The Power of Storytelling in Entrepreneurial Investing:

Storytelling conveys startup visions. We explore the art of connecting with founders' narratives and investment stories.

Conclusion:

"The Art of Entrepreneurial Investing" celebrates the transformative potential of backing early-stage companies and startups that shape the future of industries and society. Just as an artist carefully selects brushstrokes and colors to create a captivating painting, entrepreneurial investors strategically choose the ventures that have the potential to disrupt and innovate on a grand scale.

CHAPTER 45: THE ARTFUL INVESTOR'S MINDSET

Introduction:

In Chapter 45, "The Artful Investor's Mindset," we delve into the psychological and emotional aspects of investing that influence decision-making and long-term success. The artful investor's mindset goes beyond mere financial knowledge; it encompasses a set of attitudes, beliefs, and behaviors that shape one's approach to investing. This chapter explores the principles of the artful investor's mindset, strategies for cultivating a resilient and disciplined approach, and the transformative benefits of adopting a mindset that fosters growth and adaptability in the world of finance.

1. The Significance of Mindset in Investing:

The investor's mindset shapes outcomes. We discuss the importance of cultivating a positive and growth-oriented approach to investing.

2. The Art of Emotional Intelligence in Finance:

Emotional intelligence enhances decision-making. We explore the art of managing emotions and avoiding impulsive actions in investing.

3. The Influence of Risk Appetite and Tolerance:

Risk tolerance varies among investors. We discuss the art of aligning investment strategies with individual risk profiles.

4. The Power of Patience and Long-Term Vision:

Patience is a virtue in investing. We explore the art of focusing on long-term goals amid short-term market fluctuations.

5. The Art of Learning from Mistakes:

Mistakes offer valuable lessons. We discuss the art of embracing failures and using them to improve investment strategies.

6. The Influence of Behavioral Biases:

Biases influence decision-making. We explore the art of recognizing and overcoming common cognitive biases in investing.

7. The Power of Mental Models:

Mental models inform investment analysis. We discuss the art of using frameworks and models to assess investment opportunities.

8. The Art of Staying Disciplined in Market Volatility:

Discipline is essential in turbulent markets. We explore the art of adhering to investment strategies during market fluctuations.

9. The Influence of Optimism and Realism:

Optimism motivates while realism keeps investors grounded. We discuss the art of balancing positive outlooks with objective assessments.

10. The Power of Flexibility and Adaptability:

Adaptability responds to changing markets. We explore the art of adjusting strategies to evolving investment landscapes.

11. The Art of Managing FOMO and FUD:

FOMO (Fear of Missing Out) and FUD (Fear, Uncertainty, Doubt) influence investor decisions. We discuss the art of staying level-headed amid market sentiments.

12. The Influence of Mindfulness in Investing:

Mindfulness enhances focus and awareness. We explore the art of staying present and attentive in investment analysis.

13. The Power of Continuous Learning:

Learning fosters growth. We discuss the art of staying informed and educated in the ever-changing financial world.

14. The Art of Goal Setting and Visualization:

Goal setting directs investments. We explore the art of envisioning and working toward financial objectives.

15. The Influence of Confidence and Humility:

Confidence builds conviction, while humility keeps egos in check. We discuss the art of balancing self-assurance with openness to learning.

16. The Power of Maintaining an Information Edge:

Information edge enhances decision-making. We explore the art of accessing valuable insights for informed investment choices.

17. The Art of Cultivating a Supportive Network:

A supportive network enhances resilience. We discuss the art of surrounding oneself with mentors and like-minded investors.

18. The Influence of Focus and Concentration:

Focus sharpens investment analyses. We explore the art of staying attentive and avoiding distractions.

19. The Power of Turning Knowledge into Action:

Action drives results. We discuss the art of translating financial knowledge into tangible investment decisions.

20. The Art of Gratitude and Contentment:

Gratitude fosters a positive mindset. We explore the art of appreciating successes and being content with investment outcomes.

21. The Influence of Environmental Awareness:

Environmental awareness impacts investment choices. We discuss the art of considering environmental factors in portfolios.

22. The Power of Perspective and Context:

Perspective frames investment decisions. We explore the art of assessing market events in the context of long-term trends.

23. The Art of Handling Uncertainty and Ambiguity:

Uncertainty is inherent in investing. We discuss the art of managing uncertainty and making calculated risks.

24. The Influence of Visualizing Success:

Visualization fuels motivation. We explore the art of envisioning successful investment outcomes.

25. The Power of Self-Control and Delayed Gratification:

Self-control enhances financial discipline. We discuss the art of prioritizing long-term rewards over immediate gratification.

26. The Art of Analyzing Behavioral Finance:

Behavioral finance uncovers investor biases. We explore the art of integrating behavioral insights into investment decisions.

27. The Influence of a Growth Mindset:

A growth mindset embraces learning and improvement. We discuss the art of believing in the potential for continuous growth in investing.

28. The Power of Staying Grounded in Success:

Success can lead to complacency. We explore the art of maintaining humility and vigilance after successful investments.

30. The Influence of Investment Rituals:

Rituals enhance decision-making processes. We discuss the art of creating meaningful investment rituals to stay focused and disciplined.

31. The Power of Selective Listening:

Selective listening filters noise in financial markets. We explore the art of discerning valuable information from irrelevant chatter.

32. The Art of Turning Failures into Opportunities:

Failures can lead to new possibilities. We discuss the art of reframing setbacks as stepping stones to growth.

33. The Influence of Setting Realistic Expectations:

Realistic expectations temper emotions. We explore the art of establishing achievable investment goals.

34. The Power of Simplicity in Investment Strategies:

Simplicity reduces complexity in investing. We discuss the art of prioritizing straightforward strategies over convoluted ones.

35. The Art of Resisting Herd Mentality:

Herd mentality leads to groupthink. We explore the art of independent thinking in investment decision-making.

36. The Influence of Embracing Uncertainty:

Uncertainty is a constant in finance. We discuss the art of embracing the unknown and making informed choices despite it.

37. The Power of Recognizing Financial Noise:

Financial noise clouds judgment. We explore the art of filtering out distractions and staying focused on investment objectives.

38. The Art of Integrating Passion and Rationality:

Passion fuels motivation, but rationality guides decisions. We discuss the art of harmonizing emotions with analytical thinking.

39. The Influence of Curiosity in Investment Research:

Curiosity drives exploration. We explore the art of delving deep into investment research to unearth opportunities.

40. The Power of Journaling and Reflection:

Journaling aids self-awareness. We discuss the art of reflecting on investment decisions to refine strategies.

Conclusion:

"The Artful Investor's Mindset" celebrates the transformative power of cultivating a resilient, disciplined, and growth-oriented approach to investing. Just as an artist imbues a painting with intention and creativity, the artful investor consciously shapes their mindset to navigate the complexities of financial markets.

By embracing the art of investing with a mindful and strategic approach, investors can build a foundation for enduring success, foster adaptability in the face of uncertainty, and paint a portrait of financial well-being and prosperity for themselves and future generations. The canvas of investment success becomes a reflection of the artful investor's mindset, guiding their decisions on the path to financial fulfillment.

CHAPTER 46: INVESTING IN FINE ARTS AND COLLECTIBLES

Introduction:

In Chapter 46, "Investing in Fine Arts and Collectibles," we explore the world of alternative investments, where art and collectibles become valuable assets with the potential for appreciation over time. Fine arts and collectibles have been coveted for centuries, not only for their aesthetic appeal but also for their ability to preserve and grow wealth. This chapter delves into the principles of investing in art and collectibles, strategies for identifying valuable pieces, and the transformative benefits of diversifying a portfolio with tangible assets that carry cultural significance and historical value.

1. The Significance of Art and Collectibles as Investments:

Fine arts and collectibles offer tangible value. We discuss the importance of diversifying investment portfolios with tangible assets.

2. The Art Market: Understanding the Ecosystem:

The art market is dynamic and multifaceted. We explore the art of navigating auction houses, galleries, and private sales.

3. The Influence of Historical and Cultural Significance:

Historical and cultural context enhances value. We discuss the art of investing in pieces with rich provenance.

4. The Power of Art Movements and Trends:

Art movements drive demand. We explore the art of identifying trends that influence the art market.

5. The Art of Assessing Artistic Quality:

Artistic quality defines value. We discuss the art of evaluating art and collectibles based on aesthetics and craftsmanship.

6. The Influence of Art Authentication and Provenance:

Authentication ensures authenticity. We explore the art of verifying provenance and establishing the legitimacy of artworks.

7. The Power of Art Investment Indices:

Art indices gauge market performance. We discuss the art of using art investment indices as benchmarks for portfolio assessment.

8. The Art of Collectibles and Memorabilia:

Collectibles hold sentimental value. We explore the art of investing in items that resonate with collectors.

9. The Influence of Contemporary Art:

Contemporary art represents the present and future. We discuss the art of investing in works by emerging and established contemporary artists.

10. The Power of Diversification in Art Portfolios:

Diversification spreads risks. We explore the art of balancing different art styles, mediums, and artists in a portfolio.

11. The Art of Valuation and Appraisal:

Appraisal determines market value. We discuss the art of obtaining accurate valuations for art and collectibles.

12. The Influence of Art Funds and Investment Partnerships:

Art funds offer collective investment opportunities. We explore the art of participating in art investment partnerships.

13. The Power of Alternative Art Assets:

Art extends beyond paintings. We discuss the art of investing in sculptures, photography, ceramics, and other art forms.

14. The Art of Monitoring Art Market Trends:

Market trends impact value. We explore the art of staying informed about changing art market dynamics.

15. The Influence of Art Insurance and Conservation:

Insurance protects art investments. We discuss the art of safeguarding valuable artworks with comprehensive insurance coverage.

16. The Power of Investing in Emerging Artists:

Emerging artists offer growth potential. We explore the art of identifying rising talent in the art world.

17. The Art of Responsible Art Collection Management:

Collection management preserves value. We discuss the art of caring for art and collectibles to maintain their condition.

18. The Influence of Art Investment Consultancy:

Consultants offer expertise. We explore the art of seeking professional advice for art investment decisions.

19. The Power of Art Patronage:

Art patronage supports artists and cultural initiatives. We discuss the art of contributing to the art community.

20. The Art of Evaluating Art Auctions:

Auctions present investment opportunities. We explore the art of participating in art auctions strategically.

21. The Influence of Art Market Transparency:

Transparency builds investor confidence. We discuss the art of understanding market pricing and transactions.

22. The Power of Cultural and Niche Collectibles:

Niche collectibles have niche value. We explore the art of investing in cultural artifacts and unique collectibles.

23. The Art of Fine Wine and Whisky Investments:

Fine wines and whiskies mature in value. We discuss the art of investing in luxury beverages.

24. The Influence of Pop Culture and Contemporary Memorabilia:

Pop culture items appeal to collectors. We explore the art of investing in memorabilia from entertainment and sports.

25. The Power of Philanthropy through Art:

Art supports charitable causes. We discuss the art of leveraging art investments for philanthropic initiatives.

26. The Art of Investing in Rare Books and Manuscripts:

Rare books hold historical value. We explore the art of investing in literary treasures.

27. The Influence of Antique and Vintage Furniture:

Antiques hold enduring appeal. We discuss the art of investing in vintage furniture and decorative arts.

28. The Power of Sustainable Art Investing:

Sustainability aligns with responsible investing. We explore the art of supporting environmentally conscious art initiatives.

29. The Art of Art Investment Tax Planning:

Tax planning optimizes returns. We discuss the art of understanding tax implications related to art investments.

30. The Influence of Art Collateralization:

Art can be used as collateral. We explore the art of leveraging art assets for financing.

Conclusion:

"Investing in Fine Arts and Collectibles" celebrates the transformative potential of diversifying investment portfolios with tangible assets that carry cultural and historical significance. Just as an artist crafts masterpieces that endure the test of time, investors carefully select artworks and collectibles that have the potential to appreciate and preserve wealth over generations.

By embracing the art of investing in art and collectibles, investors can add a layer of richness to their portfolios, supporting artists and cultural heritage while simultaneously benefiting from the potential financial gains. The canvas of investment success becomes a tapestry of cultural appreciation, historical significance, and enduring value in the world of fine arts and collectibles.

CHAPTER 47: THE ART OF REAL ESTATE INVESTING

Introduction:

In Chapter 47, "The Art of Real Estate Investing," we explore the world of real estate as a lucrative and tangible investment avenue. Real estate has been a cornerstone of wealth building for centuries, offering the potential for passive income, appreciation, and portfolio diversification. This chapter delves into the principles of real estate investing, strategies for identifying profitable properties, and the transformative benefits of adding real estate assets to an investment portfolio.

1. The Significance of Real Estate as an Investment:

Real estate offers stability and tangible value. We discuss the importance of diversifying portfolios with physical assets.

2. The Art of Understanding Real Estate Markets:

Real estate markets vary regionally. We explore the art of analyzing market trends and local economic factors.

3. The Influence of Real Estate Cycles:

Cycles impact property values. We discuss the art of recognizing and adapting to different phases of the real estate market.

4. The Power of Property Types:

Different property types offer varying returns. We explore the art of investing in residential, commercial, industrial, and mixed-use properties.

5. The Art of Real Estate Due Diligence:

Due diligence ensures sound investments. We discuss the art of researching properties thoroughly before purchase.

6. The Influence of Real Estate Investment Strategies:

Strategies drive real estate success. We explore the art of buy-and-hold, fix-and-flip, and rental property investing.

7. The Power of Real Estate Syndications:

Syndications pool resources for larger deals. We discuss the art of participating in real estate partnerships.

8. The Art of Evaluating Rental Properties:

Rental properties generate passive income. We explore the art of assessing cash flow potential and property management.

9. The Influence of Real Estate Financing:

Financing options impact investment decisions. We discuss the art of choosing appropriate mortgage types and leverage.

10. The Power of Real Estate Tax Benefits:

Tax benefits enhance returns. We explore the art of leveraging deductions and 1031 exchanges.

11. The Art of Real Estate Property Management:

Effective management ensures profitability. We discuss the art of overseeing properties and tenant relationships.

12. The Influence of Real Estate Location:

Location drives property value. We explore the art of investing in high-demand and developing areas.

13. The Power of Real Estate Negotiation:

Negotiation impacts purchase prices. We discuss the art of securing favorable deals through effective negotiation.

14. The Art of Real Estate Risk Management:

Risk management minimizes losses. We explore the art of diversifying portfolios and preparing for unforeseen events.

15. The Influence of Real Estate Technology:

Technology enhances efficiency. We discuss the art of using real estate tech tools for property analysis and marketing.

16. The Power of Real Estate Networking:

Networking opens opportunities. We explore the art of building connections with real estate professionals.

17. The Art of Real Estate Property Flipping:

Flipping properties yields short-term gains. We discuss the art of identifying properties with potential for profitable renovations.

18. The Influence of Real Estate Legal and Regulatory Considerations:

Legal compliance protects investors. We explore the art of understanding real estate laws and regulations.

19. The Power of Real Estate Development:

Development offers high returns. We discuss the art of investing in real estate development projects.

20. The Art of Real Estate Market Timing:

Timing affects investment outcomes. We explore the art of recognizing market cycles for strategic investments.

21. The Influence of Real Estate Market Analysis:

Market analysis guides investment decisions. We discuss the art of data-driven property evaluations.

22. The Power of Real Estate Property Staging:

Staging enhances property appeal. We explore the art of presenting properties attractively to potential buyers or tenants.

23. The Art of Real Estate Portfolio Diversification:

Diversification spreads risks. We discuss the art of balancing real estate investments with other asset classes.

24. The Influence of Real Estate Sustainability:

Sustainability aligns with responsible investing. We explore the art of supporting environmentally conscious real estate projects.

25. The Power of Real Estate Investment Trusts (REITs):

REITs offer passive real estate exposure. We discuss the art of investing in publicly traded real estate companies.

26. The Art of Investing in Real Estate Crowdfunding:

Crowdfunding democratizes real estate investing. We explore the art of participating in crowdfunded property deals.

27. The Influence of Real Estate Market Research:

Research informs investment strategies. We discuss the art of staying informed about real estate market trends.

28. The Power of Real Estate Market Assessments:

Market assessments influence property choices. We explore the art of evaluating supply and demand dynamics.

29. The Art of Real Estate Asset Preservation:

Preservation maintains property value. We discuss the art of maintaining and enhancing property assets.

30. The Influence of Real Estate Exit Strategies:

Exit strategies ensure liquidity. We explore the art of planning for profitable property dispositions.

Conclusion:

"The Art of Real Estate Investing" celebrates the transformative potential of adding tangible real estate assets to an investment portfolio. Just as an artist carefully selects brushstrokes to create a captivating painting, real estate investors strategically choose properties that have the potential to appreciate and generate returns over time.

By embracing the art of real estate investing, investors can build a foundation for long-term wealth, capitalize on passive income opportunities, and paint a portrait of financial security for themselves and future generations. The canvas of investment success becomes a mosaic of diverse properties and income streams, guided by the artful investor's astute choices in the ever-evolving real estate market.

CHAPTER 48: THE ART OF INVESTMENT PARTNERSHIPS

Introduction:

In Chapter 48, "The Art of Investment Partnerships," we explore the collaborative and synergistic nature of investment partnerships, where individuals or entities come together to pool resources, share expertise, and pursue common investment goals. Investment partnerships offer opportunities for diversification, risk management, and access to specialized investment opportunities. This chapter delves into the principles of investment partnerships, strategies for forming and managing successful partnerships, and the transformative benefits of harnessing collective intelligence and resources to achieve superior investment outcomes.

1. The Significance of Investment Partnerships:

Partnerships foster collective growth. We discuss the importance of collaboration in investment endeavors.

2. The Art of Identifying Compatible Partners:

Compatible partners align goals and values. We explore the art of selecting partners with complementary strengths and expertise.

3. The Influence of Trust and Transparency:

Trust is the foundation of partnerships. We discuss the art of building and maintaining trust among partners.

4. The Power of Defined Roles and Responsibilities:

Defined roles enhance efficiency. We explore the art of assigning responsibilities based on individual strengths.

5. The Art of Aligning Investment Objectives:

Aligned objectives drive cohesion. We discuss the art of setting clear and shared investment goals.

6. The Influence of Investment Horizon and Exit Strategies:

Investment horizons impact partnerships. We explore the art of harmonizing exit strategies for collective success.

7. The Power of Risk Mitigation in Partnerships:

Risk mitigation safeguards investments. We discuss the art of diversifying risks through partnership structures.

8. The Art of Effective Communication:

Communication fosters collaboration. We explore the art of open and transparent communication among partners.

9. The Influence of Investment Partnership Agreements:

Partnership agreements establish guidelines. We discuss the art of drafting clear and comprehensive agreements.

10. The Power of Capital Contributions and Resource Sharing:

Capital contributions drive investments. We explore the art of pooling resources for greater investment capacity.

11. The Art of Leveraging Expertise and Specialization:

Expertise enhances investment strategies. We discuss the art of tapping into specialized knowledge among partners.

12. The Influence of Joint Decision-Making:

Joint decisions enhance buy-in. We explore the art of reaching consensus among partners.

13. The Power of Conflict Resolution in Partnerships:

Conflict resolution preserves harmony. We discuss the art of addressing conflicts constructively.

14. The Art of Continuous Learning and Improvement:

Learning drives partnership growth. We explore the art of

adapting to market changes and refining strategies.

15. The Influence of Performance Measurement and Accountability:

Performance measurement guides improvements. We discuss the art of holding partners accountable for results.

16. The Power of Investor Education within Partnerships:

Education fosters informed decisions. We explore the art of sharing knowledge and insights among partners.

17. The Art of Navigating Legal and Tax Implications:

Legal and tax considerations impact partnerships. We discuss the art of seeking professional advice for compliance.

18. The Influence of Cultural Alignment in Partnerships:

Cultural alignment fosters collaboration. We explore the art of embracing diversity while nurturing a cohesive partnership culture.

19. The Power of Long-Term Vision in Partnerships:

Long-term vision drives sustained growth. We discuss the art of maintaining focus on partnership goals.

20. The Art of Partnering with Institutions and Funds:

Institutions offer strategic partnerships. We explore the art of collaborating with established investment entities.

21. The Influence of ESG Integration in Partnerships:

ESG integration aligns with responsible investing. We discuss the art of incorporating environmental, social, and governance factors in partnership decisions.

22. The Power of Networking and Deal Sourcing:

Networking expands opportunities. We explore the art of accessing deals and connections through partnership networks.

23. The Art of Resilience in Challenging Times:

Resilience sustains partnerships. We discuss the art of weathering challenges and staying committed to shared goals.

24. The Influence of Diverse Investment Strategies:

Diversity enhances returns. We explore the art of combining various investment approaches within partnerships.

25. The Power of Exit Strategies and Liquidation Plans:

Exit strategies ensure liquidity. We discuss the art of planning for partnership dissolutions when necessary.

26. The Art of Balancing Flexibility and Structure:

Flexibility adapts to change, while structure provides stability. We explore the art of finding the right balance within partnerships.

27. The Influence of Philanthropic Partnerships:

Philanthropy fosters positive impact. We discuss the art of investing in social and environmental initiatives through partnerships.

28. The Power of International Investment Partnerships:

International partnerships offer global exposure. We explore the art of navigating cross-border investments.

29. The Art of Valuing Contributions and Contributions:

Appreciation builds partnership morale. We discuss the art of recognizing and valuing each partner's contributions.

30. The Influence of Legacy Planning and Succession:

Legacy planning ensures continuity. We explore the art of preparing for future leadership within partnerships.

Conclusion:

"The Art of Investment Partnerships" celebrates the transformative potential of collaboration, shared knowledge, and pooled resources in the pursuit of investment success. Just as an artist collaborates with others to create a masterpiece, investment partners unite their expertise and capital to paint a portrait of financial prosperity and growth.

Through investment partnerships, investors can leverage the power of collective intelligence, access diverse investment opportunities, and mitigate risks. Effective communication, trust, and aligned goals form the foundation of successful partnerships, allowing members to navigate challenges and celebrate shared victories together.

The canvas of investment success becomes a vibrant tapestry of diverse partnerships, each contributing unique perspectives and strengths. As partners adapt to market changes, continuously learn, and refine strategies, their collective journey evolves into a masterpiece of financial achievement.

Investment partnerships not only offer the potential for superior returns but also create a sense of camaraderie, support, and mutual growth among members. As partners work towards common goals, they sow the seeds of lasting relationships and a legacy of collaborative investing.

Ultimately, "The Art of Investment Partnerships" emphasizes that while individual investors have the power to shape their financial futures, collective efforts can create an even more profound impact on wealth generation and positive change in the world of investments. By embracing the art of partnership, investors can access a palette of possibilities, painting a canvas of success and prosperity for generations to come.

CHAPTER 49: BUILDING YOUR WEALTH GALLERY: THE PATH TO FINANCIAL FREEDOM

Introduction:

In Chapter 49, "Building Your Wealth Gallery: The Path to Financial Freedom," we embark on a journey towards financial independence and prosperity. Just as a gallery showcases diverse and valuable artworks, our wealth gallery comprises a portfolio of carefully selected financial assets and strategies. This chapter explores the principles of building wealth, strategies for setting and achieving financial goals, and the transformative benefits of taking deliberate steps on the path to financial freedom.

1. The Significance of Building Wealth:

Building wealth creates opportunities. We discuss the importance of financial security and long-term planning.

2. The Art of Setting Financial Goals:

Goals provide direction. We explore the art of defining specific and achievable financial objectives.

3. The Influence of Budgeting and Saving:

Budgeting fosters financial discipline. We discuss the art of living within means and saving for the future.

4. The Power of Compound Interest:

Compound interest accelerates growth. We explore the art of harnessing the compounding effect on investments.

5. The Art of Investing Wisely:

Investing grows wealth. We discuss the art of making informed investment choices aligned with goals.

6. The Influence of Diversification:

Diversification mitigates risks. We explore the art of spreading investments across different asset classes.

7. The Power of Managing Debt:

Debt management reduces financial burdens. We discuss the art of strategically handling debts.

8. The Art of Tax Planning:

Tax planning optimizes returns. We explore the art of using legal tax-saving strategies.

9. The Influence of Building Emergency Funds:

Emergency funds offer security. We discuss the art of preparing for unexpected financial challenges.

10. The Power of Asset Allocation:

Asset allocation balances risk and return. We explore the art of allocating investments wisely.

11. The Art of Evaluating Investment Risks:

Risk assessment informs decisions. We discuss the art of understanding and managing investment risks.

12. The Influence of Identifying Investment Time Horizons:

Time horizons guide investment choices. We explore the art of aligning investments with specific time frames.

13. The Power of Long-Term Vision:

Long-term vision drives perseverance. We discuss the art of staying committed to financial goals.

14. The Art of Cultivating Financial Knowledge:

Knowledge empowers decision-making. We explore the art of continuously learning about personal finance.

15. The Influence of Minimizing Lifestyle Inflation:

Lifestyle inflation impacts savings. We discuss the art of avoiding excessive spending as income grows.

16. The Power of Negotiating and Bargaining:

Negotiation saves money. We explore the art of securing better deals and favorable terms.

17. The Art of Embracing Frugality:

Frugality stretches resources. We discuss the art of living mindfully and spending consciously.

18. The Influence of Embracing Passive Income Streams:

Passive income sustains financial freedom. We explore the art of diversifying income sources.

19. The Power of Real Estate Investment:

Real estate generates passive income and appreciates. We discuss the art of investing in real estate strategically.

20. The Art of Entrepreneurship:

Entrepreneurship creates wealth. We explore the art of turning passion into profitable ventures.

21. The Influence of Continuous Career Development:

Career development enhances earnings. We discuss the art of investing in skills and education.

22. The Power of Mentoring and Coaching:

Mentoring offers guidance. We explore the art of seeking advice from successful individuals.

23. The Art of Charitable Giving:

Charitable giving fosters fulfillment. We discuss the art of giving back to the community.

24. The Influence of Estate Planning:

Estate planning secures legacy. We explore the art of protecting and distributing assets.

25. The Power of Financial Independence Retire Early (FIRE) Movement:

FIRE movement enables early retirement. We discuss the art of achieving financial independence sooner.

26. The Art of Balancing Present Enjoyment and Future Security:

Balance ensures well-being. We explore the art of enjoying life while securing the future.

27. The Influence of Mindfulness in Financial Decision-Making:

Mindfulness enhances financial awareness. We discuss the art of making conscious financial choices.

28. The Power of Surrounding Yourself with Supportive Networks:

Support networks offer encouragement. We explore the art of building relationships with like-minded individuals.

29. The Art of Periodic Financial Review:

Reviewing progress refines strategies. We discuss the art of assessing financial goals and adjusting plans.

30. The Influence of Inspiring Financial Role Models:

Role models offer motivation. We explore the art of learning from successful financial journeys.

Conclusion:

"Building Your Wealth Gallery: The Path to Financial Freedom" celebrates the transformative power of deliberate financial planning, prudent investment choices, and disciplined wealth-building strategies. Just as an art gallery curates diverse artworks with care and intention, we curate our wealth gallery with thoughtful financial decisions and aspirations for a better future.

By embracing the art of building wealth, individuals can embark on a path to financial independence and security. Through budgeting, saving, investing, and continuous learning, investors can create a gallery of financial assets that paint a portrait of prosperity, resilience, and freedom.

As the journey towards financial freedom unfolds, each step becomes a brushstroke on the canvas of personal finance, reflecting determination, foresight, and the pursuit of a brighter financial future. Through careful curation of our wealth gallery, we open doors to new possibilities, safeguard against unforeseen challenges, and create opportunities for ourselves and our loved ones.

The beauty of building your wealth gallery lies not only in the tangible assets but also in the sense of empowerment and control it provides. Just as a masterful artist molds their creation with precision and passion, individuals can shape their financial destiny through informed decision-making and a clear vision of their goals.

Ultimately, the path to financial freedom is a lifelong journey, and each individual's gallery will be unique and reflective of their aspirations, values, and dreams. By adopting the artful approach to building wealth, we can transform our financial landscapes, create a legacy for future generations, and enjoy the freedom to pursue our passions and make a positive impact on the world.

In conclusion, "Building Your Wealth Gallery: The Path to Financial Freedom" invites readers to pick up the brush of financial control, apply the strokes of wise investment choices, and create a masterpiece of financial independence that will inspire and uplift for generations to come.

CHAPTER 50: BECOMING A MASTERPIECE: YOUR JOURNEY AS A CREATIVE INVESTOR

Introduction:

In Chapter 50, "Becoming a Masterpiece: Your Journey as a Creative Investor," we reflect on the transformative journey you've embarked on as a creative investor. Just as artists evolve and refine their craft over time, your path as an investor has been filled with growth, learning, and the art of making astute financial decisions. This chapter celebrates your accomplishments, explores the principles that shaped your investment journey, and envisions the limitless potential that lies ahead.

1. Embracing Your Creative Investor Within:

You discovered your creative potential. We discuss the importance of embracing innovation in investing.

2. Navigating the Canvas of Financial Opportunities:

You explored diverse investment avenues. We explore the art of identifying and capitalizing on financial opportunities.

3. Unleashing the Brushstrokes of Risk and Reward:

You learned to balance risk and reward. We discuss the art of taking calculated risks for potential gains.

4. Crafting Your Investment Vision:

You formulated a vision for your financial future. We explore the art of aligning investments with personal goals.

5. Exploring the Palette of Diversification:

You diversified your portfolio. We discuss the art of spreading risks and maximizing returns through diversification.

6. Embracing the Art of Patience:

You practiced patience in volatile markets. We explore the art of long-term thinking and avoiding impulsive decisions.

7. Understanding Fundamentals: Painting a Solid Foundation:

You mastered the fundamentals of investment analysis. We discuss the art of assessing the intrinsic value of assets.

8. Navigating the Ever-Changing Market Landscape:

You adapted to market dynamics. We explore the art of staying agile in response to market shifts.

9. Embracing the Art of Contrarian Thinking:

You embraced contrarian strategies. We discuss the art of capitalizing on opportunities others may overlook.

10. Investing in Technicolor: Exploring Technology Opportunities:

You tapped into technological advancements. We explore the art of investing in disruptive technologies.

11. The Elegance of Sustainable Investing:

You invested with a sustainable mindset. We discuss the art of aligning investments with environmental and social values.

12. Mastering Asset Allocation: Balancing Act:

You optimized asset allocation. We explore the art of balancing risk and return through strategic allocation.

13. The Artistry of Value Investing:

You applied value investing principles. We discuss the art of seeking undervalued assets with growth potential.

14. Capturing Momentum: Riding Market Trends:

You capitalized on market trends. We explore the art of identifying and seizing momentum opportunities.

15. The Fine Art of Behavioral Finance:

You navigated behavioral biases. We discuss the art of making rational decisions despite emotional influences.

16. Sculpting Your Investment Portfolio:

You shaped a personalized portfolio. We explore the art of crafting a unique investment mix.

17. The Artful Science of Technical Analysis:

You analyzed market charts and trends. We discuss the art of using technical analysis to inform investment decisions.

18. Gaining Insights through Data Analytics:

You utilized data for informed choices. We explore the art of leveraging data to identify patterns and opportunities.

19. Artistic Insights from Legendary Investors:

You learned from investment legends. We discuss the art of drawing wisdom from the experiences of successful investors.

20. Investing in Global Masterpieces:

You expanded your horizons with global investments. We explore the art of accessing international markets.

21. The Emotional Palette: Managing Investment Psychology:

You navigated emotions in investing. We discuss the art of staying disciplined and focused amid market turbulence.

22. Artful Alchemy: Transforming Risk into Reward:

You harnessed risk for potential rewards. We explore the art of embracing risk intelligently.

23. The Gallery of Alternative Investments:

You explored alternative investment avenues. We discuss the art of diversifying beyond traditional assets.

24. Building a Masterpiece: Creating a Long-Term Plan:

You laid the foundation for financial success. We explore the art of planning for lasting wealth.

25. The Art of Timing: Seizing Opportunities Wisely:

You honed your timing skills. We discuss the art of identifying optimal entry and exit points.

26. Colors of Innovation: Investing in Emerging Industries:

You invested in cutting-edge industries. We explore the art of identifying and supporting emerging sectors.

27. Unconventional Brushstrokes: Alternative Investment Strategies:

You experimented with unconventional strategies. We discuss the art of exploring innovative approaches to investing.

28. The Art of Portfolio Rebalancing:

You rebalanced your portfolio strategically. We explore the art of maintaining alignment with your investment objectives.

29. Navigating the Storm: Investing in Turbulent Times:

You weathered market downturns. We discuss the art of staying resilient during challenging economic periods.

30. The Art of Portfolio Optimization:

You optimized your portfolio for performance. We explore the art of fine-tuning asset allocation and risk exposure.

Conclusion:

"Becoming a Masterpiece: Your Journey as a Creative Investor" celebrates your growth, adaptability, and resilience on the path to financial mastery. Just as artists create masterpieces with passion and dedication, you have sculpted your financial future with foresight and skill.

As you look back at your investment journey, acknowledge the moments of inspiration, the learnings from setbacks, and the art of continuous improvement. With your wealth gallery as evidence of your creative investing prowess, you stand as a testament to the power of deliberate choices, discipline, and the courage to embrace change.

Your journey as a creative investor is an ongoing masterpiece, evolving with each stroke of wisdom and each bold decision. Embrace the art of lifelong learning, as there will always be new techniques and insights to explore on your financial canvas.

As you move forward, remember the importance of setting new goals, reevaluating your strategies, and adapting to the ever-changing financial landscape. Continue to nurture your creative investor within, trusting your instincts while being mindful of risks and rewards.

Your financial gallery represents not just your accomplishments but also your potential. As you look ahead, envision a brighter future, filled with opportunities to make a positive impact on your life, your loved ones, and your community.

In your pursuit of financial freedom and independence, remember that becoming a masterpiece is not a solitary endeavor. Surround yourself with supportive networks, seek guidance from mentors, and share your knowledge with others.

As the final brushstrokes of this chapter mark the end of this book, it is only the beginning of the next chapter in your investment journey. With the art of creativity and wisdom as your guides, continue painting a life of financial abundance, fulfillment, and joy.

Congratulations on becoming a masterpiece—a creative investor who has embraced the art of investing and transformed it into a powerful force for personal growth and prosperity. May your journey be filled with joy, success, and the realization of your most cherished dreams.

The canvas is yours to shape, and your potential is limitless. Go forth and continue creating your masterpiece as a creative investor, leaving a lasting legacy for generations to come.

EPILOGUE

As we reach the end of "The Art of Profit: Investing with Creative Intelligence," we hope this journey has been as transformative and enriching for you as it has been for us. Like the final stroke on a masterpiece, the epilogue is a moment of reflection, celebration, and inspiration as we bid farewell to this chapter of learning and growth.

Throughout this book, we have explored the artistry of investing, where creativity meets intelligence to craft a path towards financial prosperity. From the canvas of financial opportunities to the brushstrokes of risk and reward, we have navigated the diverse landscape of investment strategies, unearthed the wisdom of legendary investors and explored the nuances of emerging industries.

Through each chapter, you have honed your skills as a creative investor, embracing the power of patience, mastering the art of portfolio optimization, and making astute decisions based on data, analysis, and a clear vision of your financial goals.

But beyond the knowledge gained and the strategies learned, we hope this book has ignited a spark within you—an eagerness to further explore the artful world of investing, a passion to continuously learn and adapt, and a commitment to embracing creativity and intelligence in your financial journey.

As you walk away from these pages, remember that your journey as a creative investor is a perpetual work in progress. The art of investing is not about reaching a destination but about savoring the process, cultivating financial resilience, and adapting to the ever-changing canvas of the market.

The gallery of your investments will continue to evolve, mirroring your growth as an investor and a person. Embrace the inevitable challenges and setbacks, for they will deepen your understanding and appreciation of the art of investing.

Celebrate your achievements, no matter how big or small, as they form the mosaic of your financial success. Each decision made with creativity and intelligence contributes to the overall masterpiece of your financial future.

In the spirit of creative investing, continue to explore new investment opportunities, embrace the diversity of your portfolio, and dare to challenge conventional thinking. As you grow as an investor, also share your knowledge and experiences with others, for the art of investing is enriched through collaboration and collective learning.

As you bid farewell to this book, remember that your journey as a creative investor is unique and unparalleled. The canvas is vast, and the opportunities are endless. With each investment, you shape your financial legacy and leave an indelible mark on your life and the lives of those you touch.

Your financial masterpiece is a reflection of your dreams, aspirations, and values—a portrait of the life you envision for yourself and your loved ones. So, go forth with confidence, embracing the art of investing with creative intelligence, and continue to paint a future that inspires, uplifts, and brings prosperity.

May your journey as a creative investor be filled with joy, wisdom, and the satisfaction of knowing that you have the power to create a financial masterpiece that will stand the test of time.

Thank you for being a part of this artistic exploration. As you step into the vast canvas of the investment world, remember that your potential is limitless, and your journey as a creative investor has only just begun.

Happy investing and may your financial masterpiece continue

to shine brightly as you embrace the art of profit with creative intelligence.

With warm regards,
Shah Rukh

www.ingramcontent.com/pod-product-compliance
Lightning Source LLC
Chambersburg PA
CBHW070118010626
45794CB00012B/62